EXPLORING
OUR NATIONAL PARKS
AND MONUMENTS

DEVEREUX BUTCHER

Executive Secretary, National Parks Association

Prepared Under the Auspices of the
National Parks Association

NEW YORK
OXFORD UNIVERSITY PRESS
1947

ACKNOWLEDGMENTS

The National Parks Association takes special pleasure in thanking the superintendents and custodians of the national parks and monuments for their kind assistance in verifying manuscripts; also O. A. Tomlinson, Director, Region Four; Herbert L. Evison, Chief of Information; Victor H. Cahalane, Biologist, and many other members of the National Park Service staff for their generous help. Much advice, particularly on matters of policy, was given by William P. Wharton, President, National Parks Association; also by members of the Association's Executive Committee, particularly Charles G. Woodbury, Robert F. Griggs, Edward A. Preble, Harold J. Coolidge, Jr., and Francis M. Goodwin, as well as by Fred M. Packard of the Association's executive staff. To Mrs. Devereux Butcher, who spent many weeks in assembling and arranging data, and assisted with photographic equipment on field trips, the Association is extremely grateful.

CONTENTS

Amid the supreme beauty of Great Smoky's wilderness, where the hand of man has wrought no disfigurement, Alum Cave Peaks rise to the windswept silence of high altitudes. Here a summer display of rhododendron blossoms merges into an autumn show of brilliant forest leaves.

Temples Built Not With Hands

HIGH up along the crests, rivulets are swollen with melted snow. They splash over rocks as they tumble down steep slopes to form the streams that plunge deeper and deeper into the forest below. Passing under the over-arching limbs of yellow birch and red maple, and tunneling beneath dense, dark stands of rhododendrons, the streams flow on to the lowlands to wind leisurely between mossy ledges and cliffs. Here, crowding to the banks, century-old sweet gum, gnarled beech and feathery hemlock form the forest primeval; and under-story trees—red-bud and dogwood—make splashes of pink and white. The mottled leaves of adders tongue are showing in moist places beside the streams, while on drier spots May apples are pushing green umbrellas through the brown leaves on the forest floor. The swollen streams, in their tumult, seem to echo the spirit of returning life. Spring has come to the lowlands.

As the snow disappears from the highest summits and ridges, opening buds fill the lower forest with misty green, which, day by day, climbs higher on the mountains. While the forest shade is deepening, bird songs become constant; azaleas and laurel bloom, and with them come trilliums, Jack-in-the-pulpits and pink moccasin flowers. In early summer there is the blossoming of the low country rhododendrons. Their massive clumps are arrayed with snow-white flower clusters enthroned on whorls of large, shiny leaves, lending festive dignity to the forest shade.

When warmth reaches the high country and the summits, the floral show advances, for here are yellow beardlily, woodsorrel oxalis, mountain and creeping bluets, and in some places wide-spreading carpets of sandmyrtle.

In mid-spring comes the climax display. Among scattered, dark green clumps of pointed spruces, the large, showy blossoms of pink-flowering rhododendrons spread masses of color across open ridges and summits. This is an exhibit of renown, and to see it, come people in great numbers. By the hundreds a day they come to this, their great estate.

Long after the mountains have acquired the somber greens of summer and the bright petals of rhododendrons have fallen, the people continue to come. The high country is cool in summer. All through autumn there is the added beauty of leaves turning brilliant, making the mountains blaze. Some visitors photograph or sketch the magnificent scenery; some delve into the study of birds and mammals and plants, while others ride horseback, hike the trails and camp. But whatever their activities, nearly all have the same basic purpose in coming here; they seek release from the tension of city life. The astute visitor who comes with that purpose, stays to gain renewed vigor of mind and body.

Fifty-five miles east to west and nineteen miles north to south, this public estate embraces the highest range of mountains in the East. Its name is Great Smoky Mountains National Park. More than a million people visited this park in 1946; more than had come to any national park in a single year in the history of the system. Over eight and a half million people visited all of the great parks in the same year.

It is plain to see that our wilderness reservations constitute an important phase of American life. They stand for recreation in the fullest sense, not only for pleasure and relaxation, but for the development of spiritual qualities, and to give appreciation and understanding of the forces and phenomena of nature. Every park is an outdoor university where people can come in contact with primeval nature, become acquainted with undisturbed plant and animal life, and observe the wonders of earth history. Like great cathedrals or museums of art, the parks exert deep and powerful inspirational influences. The late Dr. John C. Merriam, in speaking of the value of the parks to human experience, said, "To me the parks are not merely places to rest and exercise and learn. They are regions where one looks through the veil to meet the realities of nature and of the unfathomable power behind it."

A Unique Conservation Concept

Since 1872, when Yellowstone, our first national park, was established, succeeding Congresses and administrations have built up the system of great parks, unit by unit, in response to popular demand and in accord with certain definite standards. These standards, which have been reflected during many years in the national government, sprang directly from the people in the beginning and are vigorously upheld and defended by enlightened public opinion today. Reduced to simplest expression, the standards are based on scenery so unusual and impressive as to possess national importance, and on substantially unmodified primeval conditions of life, both plant and animal. To maintain these conditions, national park lands are exempt from commercial exploitation. The national policy allows no logging in national parks, no mining, no grazing except for former permittees, no hydroelectric development, and no open season for killing wildlife.[1]

In 1916, when the National Park Service was created the trustee of the national parks under the Department of the Interior, it assumed charge of a group of great national parks including Yosemite, Crater Lake, Glacier, Mount Rainier, Sequoia and others of that calibre. These parks were established because of their scenic magnificence and primeval quality. They met the standards exacted by the people prior to 1916, and they served as the models for future development of the system.

National Policy Defined

One of the first official attempts to define the national policy governing the parks was made in 1918 by Secretary of the Interior Franklin K. Lane. Said he: "In studying new park projects, you should seek . . . scenery of supreme and distinct quality, or some natural feature so extraordinary or unique as to be of national interest and importance. You should seek distinguished examples of typical forms of world architecture. . . . The National Park System as now constituted should not be lowered in standard, dignity and prestige by the inclusion of areas that express in less than highest terms the particular class or kind of exhibit which they represent."

A more specific definition was to come later. Originally written by the Camp Fire Club of America in 1923, and revised in 1945 by the National Parks Association, it is known as *National Primeval [2] Park Standards*. Given in full on pages 151-53, it contains, under the heading "Definition," the following statement:

"National primeval parks are spacious land and water areas essentially in their primeval condition and, in quality and beauty, so outstandingly superior to average examples of their several types as to make imperative their preservation intact and in their entirety for the enjoyment, education and inspiration of all the people for all time."

How National Parks Are Reserved

When the United States became a nation, the land that made up the thirteen colonies was established as the property of the original states. The federal government had no

---

[1] The word *wildlife*, not "game," is the proper word to use in referring to the living creatures of the national parks and monuments. "Game" is a word used by gunners to designate the species they like to kill. Since killing is not carried on in the national nature reservations, the word "game" should find no place in literature about these reservations.

[2] The use of the word *primeval* throughout this book is explained on page 149.

source of revenue in those days. Seven of the states, therefore, presented to the federal government land to found the public domain, the sale of which, in parcels to settlers and others, provided an operating income for the new government.

The public domain was enlarged during the following century by treaties with other powers, which added the Louisiana Purchase, Florida, Oregon, the vast Mexican cession, Alaska, Hawaii and other regions that, with the original thirteen states and Texas, today make up the United States of America and its territories. A large part of the land so acquired, except Texas, became federal property. This was unreserved land, given freely to the states and homesteaders, sold to prospectors, granted to railroads and disposed of in many other ways. National park lands are mostly lands that have been withdrawn from the public domain, and reserved from disposal to private interests. Some lands have been added to the parks through gift to the federal government, while other extensive acreage has been added from lands already reserved, chiefly in the national forests. The national parks are established by Acts of Congress, and only by Acts of Congress can their inviolate character be changed or their boundaries altered.

Various Kinds of Reservations

In addition to the national parks, the National Park Service, in the Department of the Interior, administers the national monuments for the protection of areas and objects of historic, prehistoric and scientific interest. It also administers national historical parks, national military parks, national battlefield sites and parks, national historic sites, national memorials, national cemeteries, and several miscellaneous areas and offices.

The Fish and Wildlife Service, also in the Department of the Interior, administers the federal wildlife refuges for the protection and restoration of native birds and mammals.

The national forests, under the jurisdiction of the Forest Service, in the Department of Agriculture, are managed in accordance with well-planned policies that provide for the commercial utilization of their resources, under conditions that guarantee an adequate supply of those resources to meet future needs. Although the actual cutting of trees on national forests is done by private concerns, the Forest Service enforces its policies of sustained yield and selective cutting, and is carrying out an extensive program of reforestation. Cattle and sheep graze under permit on some of the national forests, but care is taken to prevent depletion of the range by over-grazing. Mining and other commercial activities are permitted, and some of the largest reclamation dams have been built in these reservations. The national forests also provide many kinds of recreation. Except for certain undisturbed regions designated as wilderness and primitive areas, which are exempt from all forms of motorized transportation, the national forests are primarily commercial in character.

The states have established systems of parks, forests and wildlife refuges; but they are usually of local rather than national importance.

National Monuments

National monuments are set aside by Presidential proclamation or Congressional action, and they may be altered or abolished by Presidential or Congressional action. The power to designate federal lands as national monuments by proclamation enables the President to save areas that are in immediate danger of despoilment more quickly than is possible through Congressional action. The Act of Congress of 1906 which gave to the President this power is known as the Antiquities Act. Every President from Theodore Roosevelt to Franklin D. Roosevelt has made use of it for national benefit.

The monuments receive the same complete protection afforded the national parks. Unlike the national parks, they are not established specifically for scenery. The monuments are of many kinds. Some, such as the homes of the cliff dwellers in the Southwest, were established to save archeological remains from vandalism and theft of the artifacts that tell of ancient cultures; while others were established to preserve scientific treasures such as rare plants or animals or outstanding geologic exhibits.

Our Parks Endangered

Many people believe that when a national park or monument is established, it is thenceforth safe; but that is by no means true. Danger to the national parks and monuments comes from three main sources. There is first the pressure from industries, special interests and individuals for the commercial utilization of the resources of the area—forests, forage, waters, or minerals. Second is the pressure for establishment in the parks and monuments of artificial amusements that detract from the superlative character of the areas. Such amusements, available in urban areas and at seaside resorts, do not conform to park purposes. Third is the pressure for inclusion of inferior (substandard) areas in the National Park System that, once admitted, would lower the quality of the system as a whole.

There are approximately 600,000 acres of land within a number of the parks and monuments that are owned privately or by states. These tracts often hamper the administration of the reservations in which they occur, and create one of the most serious problems facing the National Park Service. It is difficult to discourage the owners from despoiling these lands by establishing undesirable developments, cutting forests, grazing livestock, causing soil erosion or forest fires, the effects of which may extend into park land. Every effort is being made to secure legislation for acquiring these lands.

Pressure to open the national parks and monuments to the construction of airplane landing fields is proving to be another serious problem of the National Park Service. Such construction would involve the clearing and leveling of large areas and the erection of conspicuous buildings for storage, servicing and repair of aircraft. Furthermore, flying over the parks and monuments would introduce a disturbing element that would dispel the sense of remoteness inherent in the wilderness that many people go to enjoy.

A Call for Vigilance

By comparison with our entire land area, the total of the national parks and monuments is small, comprising less than one percent of the United States, Alaska and Hawaii combined. Although Americans can well afford to reserve from commercial exploitation so small a part of their country, bills are frequently introduced to Congress to open the parks to logging, mining, grazing, flooding for irrigation and hydroelectric power, and for other despoiling activities.

It may well be asked how our great nature reservations are to be protected against such raids. There is only one way: an alert, informed public is required to see that the national policy (standards) governing the national parks and monuments is upheld. As long as the people make it understood that they want their national parks and monuments preserved inviolate for the values that they have been established to protect, so long will these nature reservations be safe from selfish exploitation. This is the concern and responsibility of every intelligent citizen, for should there come a time when the standards are lowered anywhere in the system, then will begin the deterioration of the system to the common level of playgrounds and commercialized reservations. All will be lost of this proud American heritage except a name.

[8]

NATIONAL PARKS

ACADIA NATIONAL PARK is situated on Mount Desert Island off the coast of Maine. The park includes also Schoodic Peninsula on the mainland. It is our only national park having boundaries on an ocean shore. Although established as a park in 1919, a small part of the present area became Sieur de Monts National Monument by Presidential proclamation in 1916. Mount Desert Island was discovered in 1604 by Samuel de Champlain, and in 1688 it was granted to Antoine de la Mothe Cadillac by Louis XIV of France. In 1762 it was given by Massachusetts to Sir Francis Bernard, who was governor of the colony. Within the park there are forty-two square miles of forest, lakes, mountains and rocky coast. The highest point in the park is Cadillac Mountain, 1530 feet above sea level, and this is also the highest point along our Atlantic coast. In all, there are twenty mountains comprising a range of glacier-worn granite.

Acadia's forests are of red, white and pitch pine, red and white spruce, hemlock, beech, yellow, canoe and gray birch, red maple, and, in boggy areas, white cedar and black spruce. Notable for its encircling stand of the latter is the Big Heath on the west side of the park. The Big Heath is probably the finest example of black spruce bog in the Park System. Because of much rain and the ocean-born fogs, Acadia is rich in mosses and lichens, and it has an abundance of flowering plants such as orchises, pitcherplant, the brilliant red cardinal flower and the pink lady's slipper. Deer and beaver inhabit the park, as well as such smaller mammals as the red squirrel and chipmunk. The osprey, bald eagle, ruffed grouse, cormorant, common loon, herring gull and great blue heron are among the park's larger birds; while thrushes, warblers and numerous other song birds are present during the summer. An excellent system of foot trails is maintained for those who wish to become acquainted with the beauty of the park.

Along the ocean cliffs of Acadia, pitch
pines frame views of Frenchmans Bay.

Devereux Butcher

Starfish and sea urchins are among the forms of ocean life that Acadia visitors find in rocky tidal pools. Eagle Lake, with Pemetic Mountain in the distance, is typical of Acadia's natural beauty.

Acadia Mountain, in Acadia National Park, seen here across Valley Cove from the forest of red spruce atop Flying Mountain, is one of the park's twenty mountains overlooking the Atlantic Ocean. Sphagnum moss and cladonia lichens are among the many of their kinds found in Acadia's moist forests.

In summer, when moisture conditions are favorable, Acadia's forest floor produces a wealth of mushrooms. Beauty in mushrooms reaches its height in *Clavaria flava*, one of the coral group. This species stands four or five inches tall, and is bright yellow. Its clear color and graceful formation, set in the dull colored forest floor, is a treat to behold. Propagation of mushrooms is carried on, not by seeds, but by microscopic bodies called spores. This is true also of mosses, lichens and ferns.

Photographs by Devereux Butcher
for National Parks Magazine

The elegant form and pure whiteness of *Amanita phalloides* act as a lure to the unwary person with an appetite for mushrooms. A year never passes without deaths from mushroom poisoning, and this species is the villain. Characteristics of this amanita are the bulbous base and the veil hanging below the gills; but even these distinct features cannot always be relied upon for identification. The color varies occasionally, specimens sometimes being found with a blackish or brownish tinge. This mushroom, photographed in Acadia National Park, is typical of the kind of fungi that possess gills. The many colors of mushrooms and the great variety of their shapes make a study of mushrooms a good hobby.

The great charm of the Acadia landscape lies in its unusual combination of lakes, mountains and seashore. Although there may be some small remnants of primeval forest within the park, particularly in the west side, the park can not be considered a primeval area. This being the case, it would seem all the more important to hold road building in this park to an absolute minimum. Unfortunately, this has not been done, and today most of the last wild recesses of Acadia have been opened, or are planned to be opened with roads. Actually, there are two separate road systems in the park—one for automobiles and one for horse-drawn carriages. A number of outstandingly beautiful spots in the park have thus been injured needlessly and irreparably. It is important that other national parks be guarded against this form of desecration.

Park headquarters is at Bar Harbor. Hotels and cabins are located in or near the several small towns on the island, and there are three campgrounds in the park. Acadia is reached by road on U. S. Highway 1 east from Bangor and Ellsworth, Maine, connecting with State Route 3 east of Ellsworth. State Route 3 crosses the bridge onto the island. The Schoodic Peninsula portion of the park is reached by way of Winter Harbor twenty-eight miles southeast of Ellsworth on the mainland. The Maine Central Railroad leaves visitors at Ellsworth where bus service is available to the various towns on the island. Buses also serve Ellsworth from points in New England. The park is open all year, but hotels are open only in summer.

NATURALIST AND INTERPRETIVE SERVICE is provided in most national parks, and in some national monuments. This includes conducted walks with a ranger naturalist who interprets the natural features of the areas—the geologic formations, the trees, the wild flowers and other plant life, the birds and the mammals. At many parks illustrated talks are given by ranger naturalists. These are held in the hotels or at campfires. In a number of the parks there are museums where visitors are able to learn about the areas through dioramas and other exhibits.

BIG BEND NATIONAL PARK, on the border in west Texas, was established in 1944 to protect 1106 square miles of wild desert, canyons and mountains. (It is hoped that Mexico will establish a national park across the Rio Grande, adjoining Big Bend, to form an international park.) Geologists tell us that the rock of the canyons is limestone deposited millions of years ago when the area was the bed of an ocean. They tell us,

Mariscal Canyon is one of the three spectacular
canyons carved by the Rio Grande in Big Bend.

Sierra del Carmen with its sweep of rimrock
symbolizes Big Bend's great wilderness spaces.

The Rio Grande, dividing Mexico, at left, from Big Bend National Primeval Park, flows placidly through one of its gorges.

Santa Elena Canyon, in Big Bend's southwest
corner, is seen here from a distance of a mile and
a quarter over a foreground of Texas bluebonnets.

too, that in a later geologic period the area was covered with the dense swamp forests
that were the habitat of dinosaurs. Volcanic activity belonging to a still later geologic
era is in evidence in the Chisos Mountains and elsewhere. The Rio Grande, forming the
international boundary, flows through three deep canyons—Santa Elena, Mariscal and
Boquillas—which are among the spectacular features of the reservation. The chief
mountain ranges, with their castellated rimrock, are the Chisos and the Sierra del Carmen, their highest summits nearly 8000 feet above sea level. The desert flora consists

The delicate traceries of erosion's sculpture work are typified in Bryce Canyon's bright hued Cathedral. Four people
at Cathedral's base give scale. Vegetation in the canyon is sparse, but a fine coniferous forest covers the rim.

of such interesting species as century plant, yucca, ocotillo, sotol, lecheguilla, cholla cactus, strawberry cactus, prickly pear cactus, mesquite and creosote bush. In the lower canyons, there are buckeye, hackberry, persimmon, desert willow, Apache plume and ash; while on the upper slopes there are pinyon pine, juniper, acacia and mimosa. In the higher canyons there are forests of Arizona cypress, ponderosa pine, Douglas fir and madrone— trees common to country far to the north.

Prior to the time of the park's establishment there were several large livestock ranches in the area, and the native vegetation had sufferd from grazing. How- ever, with exclusion of livestock, and under the care of the National Park Service, vegeta- tion is being restored. The wildlife of Big Bend is varied, and it includes species found in no other national park. Frogs, lizards and snakes of several kinds occur, and among the mammals there are beaver, jack-rabbit, coyote, mountain lion, black bear, kit fox, peccary (wild pigs), pronghorn antelope, mule deer and Arizona white-tail deer. The roadrunner, Mearns and scaled quail, Inca dove and cactus wren are common birds; while the Couch jay, Colima warbler, Texas blue-throated hummingbird, Mexican phainopepla and dwarf red-shafted flicker, ranging mainly to the southward, here reach their northern limits. Other birds native to the park are the painted redstart, Stephens vireo and lucifer hummingbird. In the low desert country, the rainfall is about eight inches annually, while high up in the mountains it averages about fifteen to twenty inches with some snow in winter. The summer weather is cool in the high country, but hot on the desert.

Headquarters is within the park, and the post office address is Marathon, Texas. A few housekeeping cabins are available. Hotel accommodations can be had at Alpine, 110 miles from the southwest entrance, and at Marathon, 80 miles from headquarters. Both towns are on U. S. Highway 90, and on the Southern Pacific Railroad. The park is reached from Marathon on State Route 227, and from Alpine by a county road. The park is open all year.

BRYCE CANYON NATIONAL PARK, located in wild, scenic southern Utah, was established in 1928 to preserve an area of eroded pink and white limestone and sandstone formations. The park, comprising an area of fifty-six square miles, is not strictly a canyon, but rather, an irregular cliff below which rise the beautifully colored columns that have been sculptured by rain, frost and wind. The cliff faces east. From it there is a wide view of mesas, ridges and mountains to the distant horizon. Trails for hikers and horseback riders make it possible for visitors to descend among the many-hued formations. Forests in the upper country of Bryce are mostly coniferous and include ponderosa pine, fir, golden aspen, and the rare bristlecone or foxtail pine. In the low country, slopes are sparsely covered with chaparral, pinyon pine and juniper. Mountain lion, gray fox, coyote, bobcat, mule deer, porcupine, yellow-bellied marmot, prairie dog, chipmunk and squirrel inhabit the reservation as well as many species of lizards. Bird life is abundant during the summer months.

[1] The use of the word *primeval* throughout this book is explained on page 149.

From Inspiration Point at Bryce Canyon National Primeval[1] Park one can look down upon a fantastic landscape of innumerable eroded limestone and sandstone formations that are aglow with rich color.

George A. Grant

The park is under joint administration with Zion National Primeval Park, and headquarters is at Springdale, Utah. Accommodations are available at Bryce Canyon Lodge. There is a camp center with housekeeping cabins, and a public campground. By road the park is reached from north and south on U. S. Highway 89 to State Route 12 just south of Panguitch. The Union Pacific Railroad leaves visitors at Cedar City, and the Denver and Rio Grande Western at Marysvale. The Utah Parks Company provides bus service from both points to the park. United Airlines serves Salt Lake City. The park is open throughout the year, but facilities for visitors are available only from May 10 to November 1.

CARLSBAD CAVERNS NATIONAL PARK, located near the southeastern corner of New Mexico, contains the world's largest and most spectacular limestone caverns. The area was proclaimed a national monument in 1923 and was given national park status in 1930. The explored part of the major cavern extends for twenty-three miles and has three miles of trails now open to visitors. There are three levels, the deepest being 1320 feet below ground, but only the 750 foot level is open for general visitor use. The caverns were discovered in 1901 by a local cowboy, Jim White, who was attracted to the entrance one evening by what appeared to be a cloud of smoke. Upon investigation, it was found that the cloud was not smoke, but swarms of bats leaving the cave's mouth on their nocturnal flight.

The caverns, indescribably fantastic, are made up of a series of connected rooms with beautiful calcite formations such as the Giant Dome, Crystal Springs Dome, Chandeliers and the Onyx Drapes. The largest of the rooms, The Big Room, is about 1300 feet long by 650 feet wide with the ceiling arching overhead to some 200 feet above the trail. The stalagmite and stalactite formations are the result of water seeping through the overlying limestone and consequent deposition of mineral upon evaporation of the water when reaching the open rooms. The process of building these formations is slow and fluctuates widely because of changing climatic conditions. Air temperature in the caverns remains constant at fifty-six degrees. For the convenience of visitors, the government has installed elevator service to the 750 foot level. Four hours are required to make the trip through the cavern, with an additional hour if the visitor walks to the surface by trail instead of going by elevator. The park's above-ground area contains sixty-seven square miles of desert country which, as in other national parks, is a sanctuary for wildlife and plant life. The mammal population includes the mule deer, ringtail, gray fox, coyote, rock squirrel, porcupine and an occasional mountain bobcat. Many species of birds are present, with the scaled quail, canyon wren, cactus wren, western mocking bird, pyrrhuloxia, and many kinds of hawks and owls being the most frequently seen. Among the plants are ocotillo, catclaw, mesquite, sotol, agave, gray oak, cactus and yucca.

Park headquarters is twenty-seven miles via U. S. Highway 62 southwest from Carlsbad, New Mexico. No overnight accommodations are available in the park, but these may be obtained in White's City, just outside the park boundary, as well as at Carlsbad and nearby towns on U. S. highways 62 and 283. El Paso, Texas, the nearest large city, is 153 miles west of the caverns. A branch line of the Santa Fe Railroad from Clovis, New Mexico, serves the town of Carlsbad, and the Southern Pacific Railroad serves El Paso. Bus service is available to the park from El Paso and Carlsbad. Carlsbad is on the Continental Air Line routes. The park is open all year with scheduled trips conducted daily by park guides.

CRATER LAKE NATIONAL PARK, established in 1902, is located on the summit of the forested Cascade Range in southern Oregon. Comprising 250 square miles, its chief feature is the lake lying in the crater of an extinct volcano. According to geologists, this volcano, Mount Mazama, once was 12,000 feet or more above sea level at its summit, when, thousands of years ago, it caved in after a violent eruption. The colorful cliffs, 500 to 2,000 feet in height, surrounding the lake today are all that is left of the

The calcite formations in Carlsbad Caverns are designed
by nature in infinite detail and limitless variation of
form, stimulating awe and wonderment in all who see
them. This graceful bit of ornament is in the Big Room.

Wizard Island near the West side of Crater Lake is a volcanic cone that was formed some time after the violent
eruption that brought about the collapse of Mount Mazama.

once great peak. Impressive displays of color may be found in every region of the world
and blue water is a familiar sight. In Crater Lake, however, interest is drawn and held
by an expanse of blue not exceeded in intensity or brilliance by any other lake or sea,
and by its contrast with a landscape especially fitted to emphasize these charms. Likewise, although there are many calderas throughout the world that exceed Crater Lake in
size, few if any can rival it in majesty and beauty, and none more clearly reveals the
manner in which the mountain was built, how it came to be destroyed, and how the
crater was formed. Here among the ruins of a giant volcano, nature has produced a
landscape of such extraordinary and inspiring beauty that it has been well named one
of the eight wonders of the world. Here nature has given us an unparalleled opportunity
to study her method of creation. The lake, having neither inlet nor outlet, is fed by
rain and snow. It covers an area of twenty square miles and is twenty-six miles around.

Forests of the lower country of the park are composed of Douglas fir, western yellow
pine, white fir and sugar pine, one of the largest and most handsome of all pines. In
the higher elevations such as around the crater rim, there are alpine and Shasta red fir,
whitebark pine and mountain hemlock, the latter being abundant and forming vistas
through which to view the lake. Among the park's mammals there are pine, flying,
golden-mantled ground and silver-gray squirrels, two species of chipmunks, yellow-bellied
marmot, badger, porcupine, snowshoe rabbit, pocket gopher, beaver, mountain beaver,
blacktail and mule deer and black bear. The park's birds include the golden and bald
eagle, falcon, osprey, horned owl, California gull, cormorant and Sierra grouse, as well
as a variety of song and insectivorous species such as the red-breasted nuthatch, Sierra
brown creeper, Sierra junco, mountain chickadee, western evening grosbeak, western
tanager, spotted and green-tailed towhee and Townsend's solitaire.

Crater Lake National Primeval Park, like all of the other national primeval parks
and many national monuments, is a sanctuary for wildlife. However, Crater Lake, like

At sunrise, Crater Lake is a dark blue mirror.

most of these nature reservations, is, in one respect, inadequate as a sanctuary. It provides only the summer range for certain species, particularly deer, but little or no winter range. As soon as snow falls in the park's high country, the deer are forced to migrate to lower lands outside the park in order to find winter food and to escape the severe cold of the higher altitudes. Once outside the park boundaries, they often fall prey to gunners. It is plain to see that if any one of the great parks is to be made a biotic unit, its boundaries must be extended to include both summer and winter ranges for its larger mammals. This failure to include winter range lands in the parks is the cause of many perplexing wildlife problems.

Headquarters is within the park, and the summer address is Crater Lake, Oregon. The winter address is Medford, Oregon. Crater Lake Lodge, with housekeeping cabins and store, is located near the rim. For those who bring their own equipment, there are four campgrounds in the park. Crater Lake is reached by road over U. S. Highway 97 north from Klamath Falls or south from Bend, Oregon, and over U. S. Highway 99 north from Ashland to Medford, Oregon, and thence over State Route 62 to the park. The Southern Pacific Railroad leaves visitors at Klamath Falls or Grants Pass, where bus service to the park is available from about July 1 to September 19. United Airlines serves Medford. In spite of heavy snow in winter, the park is open all year.

THE NATIONAL PARK SERVICE, created by Act of Congress on August 25, 1916, takes care of our national park system. The duty of the Service is to "promote and regulate the use of the federal areas known as national parks, monuments and reservations . . . by such means and measures as conform to the fundamental purpose of the . . . parks, monuments and reservations, which purpose is to conserve the scenery, and the natural and historic objects and the wildlife therein and to provide for the enjoyment of the same in such manner and by such means as will leave them unimpaired for the enjoyment of future generations."

GLACIER NATIONAL PARK, located in the spectacular Rockies of northwestern Montana, was set aside as a national park in 1910. Comprising an area of 1583 square miles, the reservation is one of outstandingly beautiful glacier-carved country, from which fact its name is derived. The mountains on the east side of the park resulted from the earth's crust having been lifted and forced eastward for a distance of fifteen miles. Here geologists find rock layers several hundred million years old lying above other layers many million years younger. More recently, when this part of the continent was covered by ice, vast glaciers hundreds of feet thick ground away for thousands of years to form the U-shaped valleys and the peaks that we see today. The great glaciers have vanished, but there remain in the high cirques about sixty small glaciers which are still in process of disappearing. On the west side of the park the mountains are less rugged and there is a more luxuriant forest growth because of heavier rainfall. Two hundred lakes, most of them of glacial origin, add to the beauty of the park's primeval landscape.

Forests on the east are mostly of lodgepole, limber and whitebark pines, Englemann spruce, and Douglas and alpine fir; while the forests of the west side, being in a different province of plant life, are made up of such trees as western red cedar, western hemlock, western larch, white birch, black cottonwood, western white and ponderosa pines, and grand and alpine firs, the latter with its spire-like form, characteristic of the high slopes and cirques. The white mountain goat is perhaps the best known mammal of Glacier. Other species in the park are the elk, moose, bighorn sheep, whitetail and mule deer, black and grizzly bear, mink, otter, badger, marten, coyote, beaver, hoary marmot, muskrat, red fox, pika or cony, snowshoe rabbit and porcupine. The little rabbit-like cony is an inhabitant of the many large talus slopes that occur at the bases of the sheer mountain walls. Several species of squirrel and chipmunk are abundant and friendly to visitors. Birds in the park are numerous, and include such outstanding species as common loon, red-breasted, hooded and American mergansers, osprey, bald

Hileman

On Mount Stanton, a park ranger and a group of
visitors study the effect of ancient glaciers upon the
peaks and valleys of Glacier National Primeval Park.

[23]

Devereux Butcher   A. B. Cammerer

When leaping from ledge to ledge on precipitous mountain sides, the white mountain goat in Glacier, Olympic and Mount Rainier national primeval parks provides thrills for visitors. Black bears dwell in many of the parks and are perhaps the leading wildlife attraction for visitors. In spite of the bears' seeming gentleness, many accidents have resulted from well-meaning handouts. Visitors, beware. Don't feed the bears.

and golden eagles, ruffed, Richardson and Franklin grouse, white-tailed ptarmigan, red-shafted flicker, Rocky Mountain jay, Clark crow, northern varied thrush, Alaska three-toed woodpecker, pine siskin, rufous hummingbird, water ouzel, mountain bluebird and crossbill. This park is a paradise for the botanist. Mosses and lichens abound, particularly on the west side; and in the higher elevations, there are Indian paintbrush, gentian, shooting-star, carpet pink, pentstemons, larkspur, monkey flower, glacier lily and bear grass with its conspicuous white flower clusters borne on tall stalks. Among the ferns there are parsley fern, holly fern and many others. The park has a good system of trails for horseback riders and hikers, affording opportunity to reach the rugged wilderness.

Waterton Lakes National Park in Alberta, Canada, adjoins Glacier National Primeval Park on the international border, the two areas forming the Waterton-Glacier International Peace Park. Waterton Lakes Park, considerably smaller than Glacier, contains features similar to the latter. Prince of Wales Hotel provides accommodations for visitors.

Glacier Park headquarters is at Belton, Montana. There are three hotels in the park: Glacier Park, Many Glacier and Lake McDonald; also the following chalets: Two Medicine, Granite Park, Sperry, Going-to-the-Sun and Cutbank, all in spectacular settings. There are several campgrounds, and near Many Glacier Hotel are house-keeping cabins. The hotels and chalets are open from June 15 to September 15. Glacier Park is reached by road from the east over U. S. Highway 89 from Great Falls, Montana, and from the west over U. S. Highway 2 from Kalispell, Montana. Going-to-the-Sun Highway, open to traffic after June 15 crosses the park from east to west by way of Logan Pass. The Great Northern Railroad comes directly to the west entrance at Belton and to the east entrance at Glacier Park Station, where Glacier Park Transport Company buses meet visitors from June 15 to September 15. Bus service is available from Missoula, Great Falls and Butte, Montana, and from Bonner's Ferry, Idaho. The Central

Fred H. Kiser

Lincoln Lake lies in a bowl formed by Walton Mountain, opposite, and Lincoln Peak. It is fed by a fall that plunges 1700 feet from the outlet of Lake Ellen Wilson.

[25]

The golden-mantled ground squirrel of Glacier makes friends with visitors. Because of his striped coat he is sometimes mistaken for a chipmunk. He is considerably larger, however, than the eastern and western chipmunks. Photographed at Sperry Chalets high in an alpine cirque where snow lies for nine months of the year, this one spends much of his life in hibernation. The species inhabits the forested mountain national parks, except Olympic, from California and New Mexico north to the Canadian border country.

Devereux Butcher

Throughout the United States, the mountain lion has been so persistently and systematically hunted down and shot that it is now scarce. It survives primarily only in the western national parks, and in a few national monuments and national forests. In areas where it is practically extirpated, it now contributes little to the control of elk and deer populations, which may locally become over-abundant, posing a serious problem in wildlife management. Though large, and sometimes weighing 200 pounds or more, the mountain lion is elusive. Fortunate is the park visitor who sees one.

Department of the Interior

The striking handiwork of ancient glaciers is typified in
the rocky shaft of Going-to-the-Sun Mountain at the west
end of St. Mary Lake in Glacier National Primeval Park.

Canadian Greyhound Lines buses connect at Waterton Lakes, Alberta, with Glacier Park
Transport Company buses.

GRAND CANYON NATIONAL PARK on Arizona's Coconino Plateau, is an area
of 1009 square miles. It was established in 1919. The present park area, together with
an additional portion of the canyon extending to the west, had been made a national
monument in 1908 by Presidential proclamation under authority of the Antiquities Act
of 1906. The park contains about half of the Grand Canyon of the Colorado River. A
mile deep, and varying in width from four to eighteen miles, this huge cut in the earth's
surface is the result of several million years of erosion by water. Rising from the floor
of the canyon is an array of temples, towers and castles, their intricately carved rock
walls brightly colored, predominantly red. From hour to hour the colors of the canyon
change, responding to the varying directions of sunlight, and to clouds, rain and atmospheric conditions; and contrasting with the warm colors of the cliffs and talus slopes
are the blue shadows filling deep recesses and softening the outlines of distant buttes.

The canyon's stratified rock is a fertile field for geologic study, for it is like
a book with the pages thrown open, wherein the geologist is able to read the story
of earth-building from the earliest period, the Archean, on up through the Permian
period. Here even the forms of animal and plant life that inhabited the earth during
the several periods are revealed in ancient footprints, and in the fossil remains of
the animals and plants themselves. Just as there are several life zones on mountain
ranges, so also are there various life zones in the Grand Canyon. There are four alto-
gether. At the bottom of the canyon where the weather is warm and dry, the vegetation
is similar to that of the desert of southern Arizona or Mexico where cactus, sage and
mesquite thrive on dry sites, and cottonwood trees and willows line the banks of streams.
In the cooler climate on the rim at from 6000 to 8000 feet above sea level there are
pinyon and ponderosa pine, and here in winter, snow often covers the ground.

From hour to hour the colors of the Grand Canyon change, responding to the direction of sunlight and to atmospheric conditions. Rich
blue shadows soften outlines of distant buttes and escarpments.

Among the park's mammals are mule deer, coyote, jack rabbit, ringtail,
bobcat, pronghorn antelope, badger, raccoon, striped and spotted skunks, gray fox,
as well as two handsome species of squirrel—the Kaibab, whose entire range is con-
fined to the north rim country, and the Abert on the south rim. Both of these squirrels
are large and handsome and have long ear-tufts. The Kaibab squirrel has a conspicuous
white tail. Mountain lions once were plentiful in the canyon and surrounding forests,
but organized killing outside the park boundaries has reduced their numbers. If this
large, shy and interesting native animal is to be saved within the few areas where it
still exists, informed public opinion must make itself heard. Among the birds recorded in the Grand Canyon country are golden and southern bald eagles, white-faced
glossy ibis, Gambel's quail, avocet, northern and Wilson's phalaropes, roadrunner,
Nuttall's poor-will, Pacific nighthawk, black-chinned, broad-tailed and calliope hummingbirds, long-crested, Woodhouse and pinyon jays, canyon wren, sage thrasher, chestnut-

backed and mountain bluebirds, Scott's and Bullock's orioles, lazuli bunting and Mexican crossbill. Roads lead along the canyon's pine-clad rims, and trails for horseback riders and hikers descend into the canyon. It is possible to go from rim to rim by way of a suspension bridge that spans the river in the inner gorge.

Park headquarters is on the south rim, and the address is Grand Canyon, Arizona. From June 1 to the end of September, Grand Canyon Lodge, housekeeping cabins with cafeteria, and a campground on the north rim are open for visitors. The north rim is reached by road over State Route 67, which leaves U. S. Highway 89 fifty-five miles south of Mt. Carmel, Utah, at Jacob Lake, Arizona. Visitors coming to the north rim by train, leave the Union Pacific Railroad at Cedar City, Utah, where buses of the Utah Parks Company provide transportation to the north rim, as well as to Zion and Bryce Canyon national primeval parks and Cedar Breaks National Monument. Other bus service is available from Salt Lake City, Utah, and Flagstaff, Arizona, to Jacob Lake.

The south rim is open all year, with El Tovar Hotel, Bright Angel Lodge and cabins, a camp with housekeeping cabins and a campground providing accommodations.

The little ringtail is nocturnal and is not well known to visitors. He inhabits most parks and monuments in Arizona, New Mexico, Utah, Oregon and California. Outside the parks and monuments he, and such species as raccoon, fox, skunk, squirrel, marten, mink and otter, are the victims of human vanity. Millions of wild animal pelts go into the North American fur market annually. That these creatures are disappearing from our forests, and that the steel trap used in their capture is an implement of extreme cruelty, are facts little realized by the general public. At right are the cones of limber pine, native to several nature reservations. Ranging in size from the tiny ones of northern white cedar to those of coulter pine which are sometimes thirteen inches long, cones interest many park visitors.

W. M. Rush for U. S. Forest Service   Devereux Butcher

Riding down winding trails from the pine forests on the Grand Canyon's rim to the warm, dry desert-like country in the canyon's depths is a thrilling experience for visitors. Here a group returns by the Yaki Trail.

The moose, tallest of North America's mammals, stands six feet high at the shoulder and weighs up to 1400 pounds. Seclusive and becoming scarce, he inhabits swamps and lake shores in Grand Teton, Glacier and Yellowstone national primeval parks and Jackson Hole National Monument, where he lives on water lilies and other aquatic plants. Bulls in autumn and cows with calves usually do not like intruders. Visitors should not approach too close.

PARADISE
LOST

THROUGH CARELESSNESS WITH FIRE

MADE BY WPA CCC   NATIONAL PARK SERVICE

WPA Poster   Photographed by Devereux Butcher for National Parks Magazine

Seventy percent of the forest fires in the United States each year are caused by man, and burn a total area the size of the State of Indiana. This destruction of natural beauty, forests and plants, and wildlife with its habitat, would be prevented if everybody who goes into the woods were careful. Let's keep our forests green by extinguishing camp fires and dropping no lighted matches, cigarettes or pipe tobacco along wooded trails or roads, and let's educate others to take these same important precautions.

Leigh Lake, above, in Grand Teton is said to be the most beautiful lake in the United States. From the slopes of the Teton Mountains can be seen the level floor of Jackson Hole National Monument and the Gros Ventre Mountains beyond.

George A. Gr

Middle Teton, Grand Teton, Teewinat and Mount Owens, rising abruptly 7000 feet from the floor of Jackson Hole, are among the highest peaks in Grand Teton National Primeval Park.

[34]

Phantom Ranch in the canyon offers accommodations to riders and hikers. State Route 64 connecting with U. S. Highway 66 two miles east of Williams, Arizona, runs to the south rim. State Route 64 also connects with U. S. Highway 89 at Cameron, Arizona. The Santa Fe Railroad serves Williams, and from here daily Pullman trains run to the park. Fred Harvey buses also operate between Williams and the park.

GRAND TETON NATIONAL PARK is located in scenic northwestern Wyoming, and was established in 1929 to protect 150 square miles of jagged mountains and wild forests. The northern boundary of the park is eleven miles south of Yellowstone National Primeval Park, and the northern and eastern borders adjoin the Jackson Hole National Monument. The Teton range with its spire-like peaks of pale gray rock is particularly impressive when seen across the level sage-covered flats of Jackson Hole. Standing isolated from other mountain ranges, the Tetons rise abruptly more than 7000 feet above the valley. The park's highest summit, Grand Teton, is 13,766 feet above sea level. In all, there are thirty-seven named peaks in the park, five large lakes and several small alpine lakes. According to geologists, the Tetons comprise a fault-block range. In early geologic times the rock comprising the present mountain range was broken off along a north-south line and slowly uplifted probably to a height of more than 20,000 feet above its former position. The plain along the east side of the break, Jackson Hole, was lowered, but remained fairly level. More recently, during the ice age, glaciers streamed down over the Tetons shaping them into the peaks we see today. Moraines of the glaciers are in evidence across the canyons and in Jackson Hole, where they form lakes. Such glacial lakes are Jenny, Leigh, Phelps, Taggart and Bradley.

Forests of Grand Teton National Primeval Park are composed of whitebark, limber and lodgepole pines, alpine and Douglas Fir, Engelmann and Colorado blue spruce, cottonwood and quaking aspen. The largest known whitebark pine is in this park. Moose is the most common large mammal of the area. Elk, bighorn sheep, black and grizzly bear, mule deer, marten, badger, red fox, beaver, cony, snowshoe and white-tailed jack rabbits, porcupine, muskrat, yellow-bellied marmot, coyote, mink and otter also inhabit the park. Among the birds of Grand Teton there are Barrow's golden-eye duck, American merganser, Richardson's and gray ruffed grouse, western horned owl, red-naped and Natalie's sapsuckers, Clark crow, long-tailed and mountain chickadees, water ouzel, mountain bluebird, Bohemian waxwing and lazuli bunting. In the park's four life zones there is a wide variety of flowering plants that start blooming as soon as the snow melts in spring. Visitors will find in Grand Teton a fine system of trails for hikers and horseback riders winding through the forested lower slopes and into the high peaks.

Park headquarters is within the park. The address is Moose, Wyoming. Accommodations are available at numerous privately owned ranches in Jackson Hole, and there are campgrounds in the park at Jenny Lake and String Lake. Grand Teton National Primeval Park is reached by road from the north on U. S. Highway 89 from Yellowstone National Primeval Park; from the southeast on U. S. Highway 287 from Rawlins, Wyoming, to Moran near the east entrance to the park; from the south on U. S. highways 187 and 189 from Rock Springs and Evanston, Wyoming, to Jackson near the south entrance to Jackson Hole National Monument. There is also a scenic route to the park, State Route 22, from Victor, Idaho, which crosses the Teton Mountains at Teton Pass. Yellowstone Park Company buses take visitors from Yellowstone National Primeval Park to Grand Teton National Primeval Park. Bus service is also available from Victor to Moran. There is train service to West Yellowstone and Gardner, Montana, Cody, Wyoming and Victor. The park is open from June 15 to September 15.

GREAT SMOKY MOUNTAINS NATIONAL PARK, in western North Carolina and eastern Tennessee, established and dedicated in 1940 to protect the last sizeable remnant of southern primeval hardwood forest, comprises an area of 720 square miles.

An outstanding feature of Great Smoky Mountains National
Primeval Park is its luxuriant hardwood forest, a large part
of which has never known ax or saw. Here, particularly
in the eastern end of the park, is the forest primeval.

NATIONAL PARK SERVICE
IT IS UNLAWFUL
TO INJURE SHRUBBERY
AND TREES.
TO PICK FLOWERS AND
FERNS.
TO MAR OR DEFACE ANY
OF THE NATURAL FEATURES
IN ANY NATIONAL PARK
DEPARTMENT OF THE INTERIOR

Devereux Butcher

In order that those who come next shall also enjoy, it is an imperative duty of each park visitor to protect from injury all forms of nature in the national parks and monuments.

The park contains a number of the highest mountains in the East. Several peaks are over 6000 feet above sea level, with Clingman's Dome, the highest in the park, 6643 feet. Great Smoky is comparable in grandeur and in its wilderness solitudes to many of the western parks. It represents eastern landscape and the finest of eastern forests. Its features are its spurred ridges, deep valleys, wild mountain scenery, the splendor of its flowering, its innumerable waters and its great areas of richly varied deciduous forest untouched by the ax. There are 130 species of native trees in the park, among them virgin stands of red spruce along the high ridges, and eastern hemlock, buckeye, black cherry, silverbell, yellow birch and tulip tree, the latter attaining great size. The American chestnut, once abundant here, grew to large proportions, but this fine tree has been practically exterminated by the chestnut blight. In May, June and July rhododendrons ranging from white to purple-pink make magnificent color displays along the high, open ridges as well as in the towering forests on the lower slopes. Blooms of dogwood, redbud, azalea and mountain laurel add to the park's primeval beauty.

Besides the trees and shrubs there is an abundance of flowering plants that reach their height of blossoming in late April. When the park was created, wildlife was scarce owing to killing by gunners. However, under protection, many species such as bear, deer, fox, raccoon and bobcat, as well as ruffed grouse and turkey are coming back. There are many fine trails for hiking and horseback riding. The famous Appalachian Trail which runs from Maine to Georgia passes through the park.

A few years ago the superb wilderness of this park was threatened with being split in two by a sky-line road. Eight miles of such a road was constructed to Clingman's Dome. As far as wilderness and nature preservation are concerned, road building is one of civilization's most destructive activities. If any part of North America is to remain as nature made it, the human urge to build roads must be controlled. Constant vigilance on the part of all who appreciate nature is necessary to prevent needless road building in the primeval parks and other wilderness reservations.

One of the interesting flowers of eastern forests is the Jack-in-the-pulpit. Acadia, Isle Royale, Shenandoah, Mammoth Cave and Great Smoky Mountains national parks lie within its wide range. Growing from one to three feet tall, the Jack hides its flowers around the base of its spadix inside the striped spathe. In late summer, when leaves and spathe have faded, a cluster of bright red berry-like fruit remains. The Jack is protected in the parks, but elsewhere its range is being narrowed by land-clearing for agriculture and urban development. Spring forest fires may be a very serious factor in reducing its abundance.

Photographs by Devereux Butcher

The moccasin flower or lady's slipper, blooming from May to June, is a floral gem of the East, its wide range covering the same parks as that of the Jack-in-the-pulpit. The plant consists of two leaves with a single flower stalk. The moccasin flower is the victim of its own beauty. Unthinking people cannot resist picking it, and nurserymen dig it for sale to gardeners, although when removed from its natural habitat it soon dies. Only in the national parks and in wild flower preserves is it safe today.

The great horned owl, handsomest and largest of our owls, and a valuable species in controlling over-abundance of mice, rats and ground squirrels, is needlessly killed everywhere by man except in our nature reservations. Although a resident of all the parks and monuments, he is rarely seen, for he seeks seclusion during daylight hours. His deep-toned *hoo* notes repeated four or five times are a familiar night sound in forests and deserts alike.

Dale Sanders for
U. S. Forest Service

The bobcat, like the mountain lion and its nearest relative the lynx, is ruthlessly pursued and killed by man, both as a predator and as a furbearer. He is a resident of nearly all the national parks and national nature monuments, and only there does he find safety from his greatest enemy, man. The lynx, a larger cat, has a range limited to the north, where it inhabits Glacier, Mount Rainier and Yellowstone. Perhaps the greatest contribution that the parks and monuments are making toward wildlife preservation is in showing millions of people each year that pleasure from wildlife comes not from killing, but from observing it.

Lloyd F. Ryan for
U. S. Forest Service

[39]

National Park Service

In spring and summer thousands of visitors are attracted to the Great Smoky Mountains by the pink-flowered rhododendrons, which spread masses of color among spire-pointed spruces along high summits and ridges.

Great Smoky headquarters is at Gatlinburg, Tennessee. Accommodations within the park are available from June through August at the Wonderland Club Hotel within the park at Elkmont on State Route 73, which runs between Gatlinburg and Maryville, Tennessee; and from May 15 to October 15 at Mount LeConte Lodge on the summit of Mount LeConte. The latter can be reached only on foot or horseback. There are campgrounds at Smokemont, North Carolina, and at Chimneys, Tennessee, within the park on state routes 71 and 107 which join at the state line in the park and run through the park from Knoxville, Tennessee, on the west, connecting with U. S. Highway 19 to Asheville, North Carolina, on the east. Hotel accommodations are available all year at Asheville, Gatlinburg and Knoxville. The Southern Railroad and Louisville and Nashville Railroad leave visitors at Knoxville, and the Southern Railroad at Asheville. From both towns bus service to the park is available. The park is open all year.

HAWAII NATIONAL PARK, on the Hawaiian Islands in mid-Pacific, is located partly on the Island of Hawaii and partly on the Island of Maui. The two areas total 270 square miles, and were established as a national park in 1916 to protect not only the volcanic wonders, but also its fauna and tropical forests. There are three volcanos in the park. These are Mauna Loa, 13,680 feet above sea level, and Kilauea, 4000 feet above sea level, on the Island of Hawaii; and Haleakala, 10,032 feet above sea level, on the Island of Maui. Mauna Loa is active approximately every four years, while nearby Kilauea also erupts frequently. Such regular and frequent volcanic activity lends unusual interest to this park. The crater of Kilauea often contains a lake of lava that hisses and rumbles and boils like geysers, and after sundown it makes a spectacular display, for it is then that its seething mass of molten lava and flames with their bright colors of red, orange, purple, green and blue can best be appreciated. The summit of Mauna Loa, though hot inside, is covered with snow part of the year. Haleakala, now dormant for 200 years, has a crater a thousand feet deep, seven miles long and three wide.

Kilauea Volcano in Hawaii National Primeval Park presents an awe-inspiring exhibit of volcanic activity when it erupts about once a year.

K. Maehara

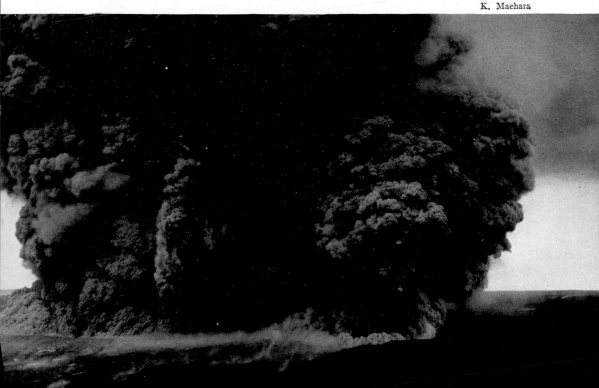

Pan-Pacific Press Bureau, courtesy Nature Magazine

The road to Kilauea Volcano in Hawaii National Primeval Park passes through a forest of tree ferns, a feature of outstanding interest to visitors. The ferns attain heights up to forty feet and have fronds twenty-five feet long.

Hawaii National Primeval Park contains a jungle of tree ferns. These ferns attain heights of up to forty feet, and their fronds are twenty-five feet in length. The handsome ohia tree adds to the striking beauty of this fern forest. Taller than the ferns, and spreading above them, this tree has gray-green leaves and brilliant red blossoms called "lehua," and designated as the flower of the islands. Hawaiian mahogany, or koa, and sandalwood are other trees of great beauty in the park. Among the flowering plants is the silversword, which grows nowhere else in the world. In the park it is found only in the crater of Haleakala. Resembling the yuccas of Arizona and New Mexico, it has narrow silvery leaves and a cluster of purple flowers borne at the top of a tall stalk. This plant, like the century plant, blooms but once during its life. The silversword, together with much of the original vegetation of the park, has suffered from grazing goats which were imported to the islands many years before the park was established. In order to restore, in so far as possible, the natural plant life of the area, every effort has been made to keep the goats out of the park during recent years. Unfortunately there has been considerable importation of exotic species of birds to the islands. A few of the more important native species are the akiapolaau, a brown and white thrush known as the amao, a member of the flycatcher family called the elepaio, the amakihi, and the apapane of red, black and white plumage. Most brilliant of the park's birds is the iiwi which frequents the ohia trees. The male of the iiwi is scarlet with black wings and tail and pink sickle-shaped bill. One of the rare birds of the park is the nene or Hawaiian goose which is sometimes seen on the slopes of Mauna Loa. Its rarity is due to killing by gunners prior to park establishment. For visitors who like to hike, there are 153 miles of foot trails in the park. An automobile road goes to the top of Haleakala, and a road goes part way to the summit of Mauna Loa.

Park headquarters is at Kilauea. The address is Hawaii National Park, Territory of Hawaii. Accommodations are provided for visitors at Volcano House in the Mauna Loa-Kilauea section of the park on the Island of Hawaii. Open all year, both sections of the park are reached by steamer from Honolulu.

ISLE ROYALE NATIONAL PARK was established in 1940 to protect permanently a wilderness island of 210 square miles located in waters belonging to the State of Michigan in northern Lake Superior. The island is fifty miles from the shore of

The picturesque, craggy shores of Raspberry Island
are typical of Isle Royale's rocky, broken shore lines.

W. Ray Scott, courtesy The Wilderness Society

The summit of Lookout Louise in Isle Royale affords a view of Duncan Bay and the park's forested peninsulas.

Michigan's northern peninsula, and twenty miles from the Canadian and Minnesota shores. According to geologists, the island was submerged for many years after the great ice sheet receded, finally appearing after the level of the lake had fallen. The shores are rocky, with caves and high jagged cliffs. The island, forty-five miles in length and, at its greatest width, nine miles wide, has a number of lakes and several narrow bays reaching far inland. The forest growth is dense, with balsam fir as the dominant coniferous species. There are also white cedar, white and black spruce, tamarack, red, white and jack pine, trailing juniper, white, black and yellow birch, striped, red and sugar maple, black ash, and northern red oak. Flowering plants in woods and bogs are numerous, including such species as bunchberry, Labrador tea, pipsissewa, twin-flower, pitcher plant, trillium, one-flowered pyrola and several kinds of orchises. There is also an abundance of mosses, ferns, lichens and fungi. Most important mammal of the island is the moose, of which there is a considerable number. Coyote, snowshoe rabbit and beaver also inhabit Isle Royale, as well as a large number of bird species including the osprey, Canada jay, herring gull, downy and pileated woodpeckers, chicadee, American merganser, black duck, and bald eagle. There are trails to various points.

In the summer of 1936, during a period of high winds and dry weather, forty-six square miles—nearly one fourth—of Isle Royale's forests were burned. It will require more than a hundred years for that same area to return to some semblance of the original primeval forest. The destruction of plant and wildlife habitat, and the loss of natural beauty, are complete when brought about by fire. To prevent this kind of desecration in the National Park System during dry summer months, when thousands of people are in the parks, calls for constant care and vigilance on the part of every visitor.

Park headquarters is at Houghton, Michigan, in winter, and on Mott Island in Isle Royale's Rock Harbor from May to November. The address is Isle Royale National Park, via Houghton, Michigan. Rock Harbor Lodge, accommodating visitors, is located in the harbor of that name, where boats come in from Copper Harbor, Michigan, Buffalo, New York, and from Duluth and Grand Marais, Minnesota. Windigo Inn also accommodates visitors at Washington Harbor. Belle Isle Camp, on a small island off the northwest coast of Isle Royale, provides meals and has cottages for rent. The park is open from June 15 to September 15.

KINGS CANYON NATIONAL PARK. See SEQUOIA-KINGS CANYON NATIONAL PARK.

LASSEN VOLCANIC NATIONAL PARK, in northern California, was established in 1916. The area comprises 163 square miles of mountain, forest and lake country that is full of the remains of volcanic activity. Chief feature of the park is Lassen Peak, the most recently active volcano in the United States proper, which made 298 outbursts between the years 1914 and 1921. Important among the park's volcanic exhibits are Bumpas Hell, Sulphur Works and Devil's Kitchen, all three consisting of sulphur and steam fumaroles. Other exhibits are the Cinder Cone with its lava flow of 1850-51 and its barren, symmetrical slopes of loose cinders; and Chaos Crags and Chaos Jumbles, scenes of extreme desolation, which are the remains of lava domes that have been shattered by later activity. The Devastated Area is another point of interest. The conditions of this area were brought about by a blast of gas and a torrent of mud suddenly released down the northeast slope of Lassen Peak, which wiped out the forest in its path. Throughout the park there are over fifty lakes, most of them lying hidden in the wilderness or accessible by trail only. Lassen's forests consist of such conifers as whitebark, ponderosa and sugar pine, incense cedar, red and white fir and mountain hemlock. Blacktail and mule deer inhabit the park as well as numerous smaller mammals such as squirrel, marmot, cony, mink and badger. Nearly 300 species of wildflowers have been identified in the park. Along Kings Creek and Manzanita Creek the meadows are filled with wild flowers in summer. Perhaps the most interesting floral species on the reservation is the crimson snow-plant, which appears as soon as the snow melts, and remains for several weeks.

The wild flower meadows of Lassen, together with those of other national parks, especially in California, have been coveted by local livestock interests. Attempts have been made by these interests to legalize cattle grazing on the parks' meadows. Such action by the livestock interests is motivated by a desire for personal profit at the national expense. It shows their failure to recognize that the parks have been created in conformity to the will of the people for the purpose of preserving a bit of primitive landscape for the enjoyment of future generations. Grazing cattle on the parks' meadows would result in the utter destruction of the natural flora which is of interest to thousands of visitors annually. Protection of Lassen and other great parks from such destructive commercial invasion calls for constant vigilance by nature lovers everywhere.

Lassen Volcanic National Park headquarters is at Mineral, California. Accommodations are available at Manzanita Lake Lodge where there are also housekeeping cabins. There are five campgrounds for those who bring their own equipment. The park is reached by road from Redding and Red Bluff, California, on the west, over state routes 44 and 36 respectively, connecting with State Route 89, which runs through the park. It can be reached also over State Route 36 from Susanville on the east. The Southern Pacific Railroad leaves visitors at Red Bluff and Redding, and the Western Pacific Railroad at Keddie, from which points bus service operates to the park. Lassen is open during the summer months, opening and closing dates depending upon the weather.

In Lassen Volcanic, Chaos Crags was active about 500 years ago. It covered the foreground area, Chaos Jumbles, with lava fragments, and now a forest of lodgepole pine is very slowly becoming established there. The Devastated Area, below, where a torrent of mud poured down the side of Lassen Peak, wiping out the forest that covered this scene, is a result of the 1915 eruption.

George A.

C. Muller

Lassen Peak erupted intermittently from 1914 to 1921.

MAMMOTH CAVE NATIONAL PARK, in southwestern Kentucky, became fully established in 1941 to provide protection for the limestone cave of that name. So far, five levels and 150 miles of the cave have been explored. The lowest level is 360 feet below the surface. Amid the scenic effects of stalagmites, stalactites, drapery formations and the domed pits that are characteristic of this cave, there are three rivers, eight waterfalls and two lakes within the caverns. The pits are a hundred feet deep with domes rising above them to a height of approximately forty-eight feet. Of great beauty are the gypsum formations of Mammoth Cave. These occur in such forms as needles, woolly masses, flower-like growths, pendants and coils of whitish translucent crystals. Though the predominant color of the cave is gray, much of it is tinted red, yellow and purple by manganese and iron oxide. The air within the cave is always fresh, remaining at fifty-four degrees. Bats inhabit the cave in large numbers. Here, too, dwells the cave cricket, and in the subterranean lakes and streams are found the eyeless cave fish and the cave crawfish. The Park Service conducts three or four trips of varying length through the cave each day. For visitors taking the all-day trip of seven and a half hours, lunch is served in the Snowball Dining Room, 267 feet underground.

The above-ground area comprises seventy-eight square miles. Hilly and forested, it is traversed by the Green and Nolin rivers, tributaries of the Ohio River. Although the park's forests are not primeval, there are many large trees in the river bottomlands. Trees of the reservation are mostly hardwood species, and include shagbark hickory, beech, sugar and red maple, black gum, yellow poplar, white ash, sycamore, American elm, sassafras and black willow. Mountain laurel adds its blooms to the spring floral display of shadbush dogwood and redbud. Important among the park's wild flowers and ferns are Solomon seal, wake robin, May apple, twinleaf, bloodroot, jack-in-the-pulpit, polypody fern, purple cliff brake and the interesting walking fern. Red and gray fox, eastern woodchuck, muskrat, skunk, mink, opossum, raccoon, cottontail rabbit, chipmunk, weasel and three species of squirrels—the gray, fox and flying—also inhabit the park. More than 170 species of birds have been recorded. These include eastern bob-white, spotted sandpiper, yellow-billed and black-billed cuckoo, screech and northern barred owl, chuck-will's-widow, eastern whip-poor-will, northern flicker and the large, spectacular pileated woodpecker.

There is boating on the park's rivers. Powerboats come up from the Ohio River, and these, as well as outboard motors, are used within the park. Unfortunately the outboard motor, in particular, has perhaps no equal as a disturbing influence to people

Roaring River, in the eternal darkness of
Mammoth Cave, is inhabited by eyeless fish.

National Park Service, courtesy The Wilderness Society

The walls and roof of Mammoth Cave are decorated with delicate, translucent gypsum crystals resembling flowers, coils and ribbons.

wishing to enjoy the quiet and beauty of nature. Since the national parks serve primarily as sanctuaries for the study and enjoyment of nature, it is sometimes seriously questioned whether power craft of this kind should be permitted within a national park.

Headquarters is within the park. The address is Mammoth Cave, Kentucky. Mammoth Cave Hotel, open all year, with cabins for rent during the summer only, provides accommodations. The park is reached by road over U. S. Highway 31W south from Louisville to Cave City, Kentucky, or north from Nashville, Tennessee. From Cave City, State Route 70 runs to the park, a distance of eleven miles. The Louisville and Nashville Railroad and Greyhound Bus Lines operate to Cave City where taxis are available to the park. The park is open all year.

MESA VERDE NATIONAL PARK, in extreme southwestern Colorado, was established in 1906 to protect the finest prehistoric Indian cliff dwellings in this country; also, splendid examples of prehistoric pit houses and surface pueblo dwellings. The park, consisting of a mesa gashed by many deep canyons and standing about 2000 feet above the surrounding plain, comprises an area of eighty square miles. Largest of the cliff dwellings is Cliff Palace, which contains more than 200 living rooms, twenty-three kivas, and eight floor levels—all within a single cave. Another large cliff dwelling group in a remarkable state of preservation is Spruce Tree House with 114 rooms and eight kivas. Scattered throughout the twenty large canyons and the numerous small side canyons are many hundreds of ruins.

The area was occupied from about 1 A. D. until about 1300 A. D., when the inhabitants were forced to leave because of protracted drought. For the first 700 years of this period the Indians are known as the Basket Makers; during the later part of the occupation they are called Pueblo Indians because of the pueblo-building

Cliff Palace is the largest of Mesa Verde's many hundred prehistoric Indian cliff dwelling ruins. These ruins constitute one of the most outstanding records of prehistoric man in the western hemisphere.

Bradford Washburn

Mount McKinley, highest peak in North America, is seen here from the northeast
showing Muldrow Glacier and its two tributary glaciers, Brooks and Traleika.

custom that developed. The story of these Indians, their skills in the arts and crafts,
their methods of building and agriculture, as reconstructed, provides an absorbing study
for those interested in catching a glimpse of North America's prehistoric civilization.

Inhabiting the park are such mammals as the Rocky Mountain mule deer, black
bear, fox, coyote, bobcat, badger, porcupine, prairie dog, and chipmunk. The area
lately has been experimentally restocked with Rocky Mountain bighorn sheep and the
Merriam wild turkey which formerly lived there. The dense forest cover is composed
chiefly of Utah juniper, pinyon pine, and scrub oak, augmented by such flowering
shrubs as serviceberry, antelope brush, mountain mahogany and mock orange. Wildflowers are abundant in spring and fall.

Headquarters is in the park, and the address is Mesa Verde National Park, Colorado.
At Spruce Tree Lodge there are cabins and meals available from May 15 to October
15, as well as housekeeping cabins and tents. A free, modern campground is located
near park headquarters and is open during nonfreezing weather—about May 1 to November 1. The park entrance is located on U. S. Highway 160 halfway between Mancos
and Cortez, Colorado, and is twenty miles from park headquarters. The Denver
and Rio Grande Western Railroad runs to Grand Junction, Montrose, and Durango,
Colorado; the Santa Fe Railroad to Gallup, New Mexico. Daily bus service to the park
is provided from these and other points. Bus transportation between the park entrance
and park headquarters is not available on Sundays during the non-travel season. The
park is open from May 15 to October 15.

KILLING OF WILDLIFE in the national parks is prohibited. Nearly every one of the
acts of Congress establishing national parks contains the statement "That all hunting
or the killing, wounding, or capturing at any time of any bird or wild animal,
except dangerous animals when it is necessary to prevent them from destroying
human lives or inflicting personal injury, is prohibited within the limits of said park."

[51]

Three important mammals of Mount McKinley Park are the grizzly bear, the wolf and the handsome white Dall sheep. When seen by visitors, all three are a great source of pleasure. Since the sheep comprises part of the natural diet of the wolf, gunners have urged extermination of the wolf, both in and out of the park. To kill off any native wildlife species in a national park or monument is contrary to the national policy governing these great reservations which are owned by everyone.

Photographs by Adolph Murie,
courtesy The Wilderness Society

MOUNT MCKINLEY NATIONAL PARK, in the central Alaska wilderness, was established in 1917 to preserve 3030 square miles of the primeval landscape and protect the wildlife of the area. Unlike most of the primeval parks, this one has but little forest land. Trees and shrubs clothe the valleys and slopes below 3000 feet altitude, but a large portion of the park above that altitude is grassy tundra, while all the rest is bare rock, or snow and ice. Along the south side of the park is the Alaska Range, from which rises the highest peak on the continent of North America, Mount McKinley—called Denali by the Indians—20,300 feet above sea level. The upper two thirds of Mount McKinley are always covered with snow and ice. Muldrow Glacier, descending from the northeast flank of the mountain, is thirty miles long, and is the largest of many glaciers.

Black spruce is the most abundant of the park's evergreen trees. White spruce and tamarack are found here also, as well as black cottonwood, quaking aspen, paper birch and willow, the latter going high on the slopes and becoming small in size. In the valleys there are dwarf birch, Labrador tea, blueberry, bearberry and wild rose. Wild flowers of the park include larkspur, valerium, bluebells, monkshood, bunchberry, pyrola, twinflower, crowberry, purple vetch, lemon yellow arctic poppy and water willow which has large cerise flowers. In summer, when these plants are in bloom, the days are warm and sunny, with the temperature ranging from sixty to eighty degrees. In winter the thermometer drops to as low as fifty degrees below zero at times, but averages from five to ten below, with snow twenty inches deep. Like the other primeval parks, Mount

McKinley is a wildlife preserve. Important mammals found here are the white Dall sheep, caribou, moose, Toklat grizzly bear, wolf, wolverine, red fox, marmot, parka squirrel, porcupine, lynx, coyote, beaver, marten, mink, snowshoe rabbit and cony.

This is the only U. S. owned park where caribou and wolves occur today. The caribou has been shot and nearly exterminated over a large part of its North American range, but large herds still survive in this part of Alaska. The wolf, one of the most interesting species of native fauna, has been nearly exterminated throughout North America. It is still trapped and shot in Alaska, finding a haven of safety from its greatest enemy, man, in this park alone. Although the wolf is vanishing rapidly, there is frequent pressure on the part of gunners to have it wiped out completely, even within the park. This is because the Dall sheep, highly prized as a target by the gunners, serves also as part of the natural prey of the wolf. Thus, the gunner regards the wolf as a competitor. The expression of public disapproval of wolf extermination is constantly needed if the species is to be saved. Among the birds of the park there are the willow ptarmigan and the rare surfbird, which nests here and nowhere else in the world. There are also the yellow-billed loon, whistling swan, lesser snow goose, western harlequin and old-squaw ducks, golden and bald eagles, little brown crane, Pacific golden plover, wandering tattler, long-tailed jaeger, arctic tern, snowy owl, Alaska three-toed woodpecker and Bohemian waxwing.

Headquarters is within the park. The address is McKinley Park, Alaska. Accommodations are available at Mount McKinley Park Hotel near the railroad station at the eastern end of the park, and at Camp Eielson, a tent camp, sixty-six miles west along the park highway. The Alaska railroad serves the park from Seward on the coast, 348 miles distant, and Fairbanks, 123 miles away. Boats of the Alaska Steamship Company, plying the scenic coastal route north from Seattle, Washington, stop at Seward. The park is open from June 10 to September 15.

MOUNT RAINIER NATIONAL PARK is a superbly scenic wilderness region in Washington's Cascade Mountains. Established in 1899, and comprising an area of 377 square miles, the park's chief feature is the snow-covered Mount Rainier, 14,408

The purple-pink shooting star is one of the many floral gems of the national park alpine meadows. Among the rock slides at the bases of cliffs lives the little rabbit-like cony.

Devereux Butcher

Devereux Butcher for National Parks Magazine

**In the sunshine of late afternoon, summer clouds
weave around the snowy dome of Mount Rainier.**

feet above sea level, which contains the largest single-peak glacier system in the United States. Towering majestically above the surrounding country, the white dome of the mountain is visible for a hundred miles in every direction. On the mountain there are twenty-five glaciers that vary from fifty to 500 feet in thickness, and cover an area of about forty square miles. They recede a little each year. Mount Rainier is an extinct volcano. Some geologists think that at one time far back in geologic history the mountain may have been as high as 16,000 feet, and that an eruption blew off the upper 2000 feet, lowering it to its present elevation. The year 1870 was an eventful one for

The mine entrance in Mount Rainier, and the destroyed forest in Olympic, are examples of the despoilment sometimes carried on by owners of the 625,000 acres of private in-holdings remaining within the parks and monuments. Private lands hamper protection of the reservations, and pose serious administrative problems. This can be remedied by donation or exchange of the lands to the federal government, or by Congressional appropriations for their purchase and incorporation into the national parks and monuments.

Mount Rainier. In that year its last feeble outburst of volcanic activity occurred, and in that year the summit was first scaled by man. Traces of volcanic activity are still present in the mountain, as shown by hot springs at its foot and by steam vents in the crater. Sunrises and sunsets coloring Rainier's snowmass afford one of the most impressive sights in the National Park System. Within the park there are 240 miles of trails with shelters for hikers located at convenient places.

Some of the more important trees of Mount Rainier's forests are the Douglas fir, western and mountain hemlock, western yew, western red and Alaska yellow cedar grand, silver, noble and alpine fir, whitebark and western white pine and Englemann spruce. Whitebark pine and alpine fir grow in picturesque clumps in the high alpine

Flower carpets in the alpine meadows of Mount Rainier and other parks
are enjoyed by thousands of visitors. Livestock interests have urged
opening the parks to grazing and feeding these flowers to cattle.

country. The mountain hemlock, also a high altitude species, is one of the most
beautiful of all North American trees. Among the wild flowers of the park are the white
avalanche fawnlily, which grows in the alpine meadows and comes out as the snow
melts in spring. There are bright orange, scarlet and magenta paintedcups, red and
cream mountainheaths, blue lupine and the tiny Lyall lupine not over three inches high,
having downy leaves and a cluster of blue flowers. Inhabiting the park are black bear,
mountain goat, elk, blacktail deer, coyote, raccoon, red fox, marten, beaver, marmot,
porcupine, cony, snowshoe rabbit and several species of squirrels. Mountain beaver,
a rodent about the size of a muskrat, but with almost no tail, and a distant relative of
the common beaver, also lives in the park's moist, cool meadows and woodlands. The

bird enthusiast finds Rainier a fertile area. Among the many birds that live here are the sooty grouse, white-tailed ptarmigan, bandtailed pigeon, golden and bald eagle, several owls including the saw-whet and the pigmy, several members of the woodpecker group including the Alaska three-toed and the Lewis, Vaux swift, rufous hummingbird, Steller jay, northern raven, Clark crow, white-winged and Sitka crossbill, Hepburn rosy finch, western tanager, northern violet-green swallow and water ouzel.

Mount Rainier National Primeval Park is one of our great national nature reservations in which are located tracts of privately owned land. Such privately owned land within the park and monuments constitutes a serious threat to the protection of the areas, because it is difficult to persuade owners not to develop it in any way they wish—cut the trees, develop mines, graze livestock or establish beer and dance halls and tourist accommodations. Such activity is inconsistent with park policy and purpose, and the existence of these tracts hinders effective administration wherever they occur. Elimination of private lands will be brought about when a united public urges Congress to appropriate funds for their purchase by the federal government. In 1945, one such tract nearly brought disaster to 300 acres of Mount Rainier's forests. The owners of the tract threatened to sell out to a lumber company. Sale to the logging firm was narrowly averted when funds became available for acquisition by the government, resulting in the incorporation of the tract into the national park.

Mount Rainier headquarters is at Longmire, Washington. Visitor accommodations are provided in Paradise Valley at Paradise Inn and Paradise Lodge. At Longmire there are cabins; at Ohanapecosh there are a lodge, housekeeping cabins and a store, and at the Yakima Park area there is a cafeteria. In addition, there are numerous campgrounds in the park. Mount Rainier is reached by road over U. S. Highway 410 from Tacoma, and from Seattle over State Route 5, which joins U. S. Highway 410 at Enumclaw. Both the White River and the Carbon River entrances are reached by this route. The Longmire entrance is reached over State Route 5 from Tacoma. From

Around a campfire that scents the air with fragrant wood smoke, campers breakfast in Mount Rainier's wilderness.

Padilla Studios

George A. Grant

Sitka spruce grows big in the rain forest of Olympic National Primeval Park. Although this is one of the most magnificent remnants of primeval forest in North America, local lumber interests are seeking to destroy it.

Yakima, Washington, the park is reached over U. S. Highway 410 from the east. Buses of the Rainier National Park Company provide service from Seattle and Tacoma to Longmire and Paradise Valley throughout the year, and in summer from Tacoma, Seattle and Yakima to Yakima Park as well. The Great Northern, Northern Pacific and Union Pacific railroads serve Tacoma and Seattle. The Northern Pacific serves Yakima.

Devereux Butcher

Rainfall on the west slopes of the Olympic Mountains averages 142 inches a year, producing a forest of huge proportions where moss covers twig, limb, trunk and ground, and ferns decorate every fallen tree. Two species of ferns in this forest are the deer fern, shown with tall spore-bearing frond, and the western maidenhair.

Devereux Butcher for National Parks Magazine

Olympic's high country is a land of glacier-carved peaks and alpine
meadows and lakes. This view shows Mount Seattle in the distance.

OLYMPIC NATIONAL PARK, a nearly roadless primeval wilderness of 1321
square miles overlooking the Pacific Ocean, was established as a national park in 1938.
In 1909, part of the area had been made a national monument, but all of the monument
is now included in the park. Located on Washington's Olympic Peninsula, the park
comprises a rugged mountain mass. The peaks, of which Mount Olympus, 7923 feet
above sea level, is the highest, are glacier-carved, with their lower slopes clothed in a
magnificent forest of conifers. On the westward-facing slopes, which are exposed to

the rain clouds that drift in from the ocean's warm Japan Current, is the great Olympic rain forest. Here there is an annual average precipitation of 142 inches which produces a forest of fantastic appearance and of huge proportions.

Dominant trees are Sitka spruce, Douglas and silver fir, western red cedar and western and mountain hemlock. The largest tree in the park is a western red cedar. The largest of its kind known, this tree has a trunk diameter of twenty feet at four feet above the ground. One Douglas fir in the park has a diameter of seventeen feet eight inches, and many trees in the park reach a height of 200 feet. Dripping with rain, and with ground, trunk and limb cloaked in moss, this forest displays a great variety of greens even on the grayest of days. It constitutes one of the most outstanding exhibits of nature on the continent of North America. On the eastern and northern slopes of the Olympic Mountains, rhododendron, madrone and cascara are abundant; while the alpine meadows of the high elevations are gardens of wild flowers during summer. Among the ferns, there are sword fern, western maidenhair and deer fern, the two latter being perhaps the most beautiful of all North American species. Olympic is the home of the Roosevelt elk. Inhabiting the park also are blacktail deer, snowshoe rabbit, black bear, beaver, mountain beaver and mountain lion.

This primeval park, now preserved for the enjoyment of future generations, has been coveted by local lumber mills. These mills, having exploited the forests outside the park boundaries with little or no thought for future lumber needs, have made a number of attempts to break into the park and destroy the forests there. Public opinion has stood rigidly opposed to such desecration. Local mining interests likewise seek to invade this superb reservation. Only by the constant vigilance of an informed public can despoiling activities like these be prevented. Privately owned lands within the park cause serious administrative difficulties for rangers trying to protect the reservation.

Park headquarters is at Port Angeles. The address is Olympic National Park, Port Angeles, Washington. Within the park the following hotels provide accommodations for visitors: Lake Crescent Lodge, Rosemary Inn, Storm King Inn, Ovington's and Graves Creek Inn. Cabins at many locations are also available, as well as campgrounds, and shelters along the main trails. Outside the park there are hotels and

Picnic areas in the national parks, like this one beside Crescent Lake in Olympic National Primeval Park, are accessible by road and are equipped with tables, benches, fireplaces and sanitary facilities.

Devereux Butcher

A superb beauty spot of the Olympic Mountains is alpine Heart Lake shown in the view above. The largest surviving herd of Roosevelt elk inhabits the Olympic wilderness. Gunners and advancing civilization have extirpated this fine animal from most of its former range.

George A. Grant

Dream Lake nestles serenely below Hallett's Peak, right, and Flattop in Rocky Mountain National Primeval Park, a favorite haunt of campers and hikers.

cabin camps at Port Angeles, Forks, Aberdeen, Hoquiam, Hoodsport, Port Townsend, Sequim, Queets and Quinault, the latter overlooking Lake Quinault at the southwest corner of the park. The park is reached by ferry from Seattle and Edmunds, Washington, and from Victoria, British Columbia, to Port Angeles or Port Ludlow. The Olympic Highway, which is part of U. S. Highway 101 encircling the park, is reached from Olympia and Aberdeen. The park is open all year.

ROCKY MOUNTAIN NATIONAL PARK was established in 1915. The area, located in northern Colorado's snow-capped Rocky Mountains, is 405 square miles in extent. It contains sixty-five named peaks of 10,000 feet altitude and over, with Longs Peak the highest, 14,255 feet above sea level. The park is dotted with lakes, of which most are

The Twin Sisters, Estes Cone and Beaver Park are features in the wild
and inspiring landscape of Rocky Mountain National Primeval Park.

glacial in origin, a few having been created by beavers. In the canyons and along the streams on the east side of the park grows the beautiful and comparatively rare Colorado blue spruce. Ponderosa pine and Douglas fir are other notable trees of the park; while in the higher altitudes there are limber pine, Englemann spruce and alpine fir. Quaking aspen is one of the most abundant trees on the reservation. Over large areas in canyons and on lower slopes, it forms pure stands, and here its light colored trunks in winter offer contrast to the somber forests of evergreen. In autumn the leaves of the aspen turn brilliant yellow, making a spectacular display on the mountains. In summer the alpine meadows of this park are bright with such flowers as gentians, pentstemons, and lilies. Blue columbine, the state flower of Colorado, is found at lower elevations. The forests and meadows are inhabited by elk, mule deer, Rocky Mountain bighorn sheep, bobcat, black bear, coyote, marten, mink, badger, porcupine, muskrat, Fremont and Abert squirrels, Say's ground squirrel, beaver, marmot and cony.

Besides the geologic, botanic, and other interests of the park, the area is a paradise for the bird enthusiast. The list of migrants and permanent residents is long. Outstanding among the many species are several ducks such as the gadwall, green-winged and blue-winged teals, ring-neck duck, redhead duck, golden eagle, Wilson's phalarope, Howell's nighthawk, northern white-throated swift, broad-tailed humming-bird, Rocky Mountain and long-crested jays, water ouzel, ptarmigan, rosy finch, chest-nut-backed and mountain bluebirds, yellow-headed blackbird and western tanager.

The Congressional Act establishing this park contained a provision to allow the United States Reclamation Service to "enter upon and utilize for flowage or other purposes any area within said park. . . ." The result is that recently a water-diversion tunnel has been constructed beneath the park to carry water from the west side of the continental divide to the east side for irrigation of crop lands outside the park. Friends of wilderness and nature preservation won a victory in this case, for it is through

Fred M. Packard

In late spring, the elk at Rocky Mountain National Primeval
Park are shedding their winter coats and grazing on the
grasses of their winter range. Soon they will migrate to their
high summer pastures amid glades of alpine fir, and to the
rolling tundra above timberline. Then the mule deer fawns
appear in the forest, and the white-tailed ptarmigan cackle in
courtship on the peaks. Black scars on the aspen trunks above,
are caused by elk chewing bark when snow is deep in winter.

Fred M. Packard

their efforts that both ends of the tunnel are outside of park boundaries, and certain power lines have been routed outside the park also. However, the provision established one more precedent dangerous to the future integrity of the entire National Park System.

Park headquarters is at Estes Park, Colorado. Accommodations within the park are available at Bear Lake Lodge, Grand Lake Lodge, Forest Inn, Camp Woods, Brinwood Hotel, and Sprague's Lodge. In addition, there are six campgrounds. All are open during the summer months. At the villages of Estes Park and Grand Lake, located close to the park boundaries, as well as at privately owned establishments within the park, there are accommodations available all year. U. S. Highway 34 runs through the park. The park is reached on the east from Denver, Greeley and Fort Collins, and on the west from Granby, Colorado. The Chicago, Burlington and Quincy Railroad provides direct service from Chicago to Denver; the Union Pacific Railroad leaves visitors at Denver or Greeley, and the Denver and Rio Grande Western Railroad at Granby, from which points the Rocky Mountain Motor Company provides bus service to the park during the summer travel season. Most of the park is open all year.

SEQUOIA-KINGS CANYON NATIONAL PARK, situated on the west slope of the Sierra Nevada of California, is actually two adjoining national primeval parks. The Sequoia Park area was established in 1890 to preserve thirty-two groves of the *Sequoia gigantea* which were then in imminent danger of destruction by ax, saw and dynamite. Since 1890 the park has been enlarged until today it comprises 604 square miles of mountain and forest wilderness. The mountains of the park are glacier-carved, and rise to 14,494 feet at the summit of Mt. Whitney. This is the highest mountain in the United States proper, being overtopped by Mount McKinley in Alaska. Five caves in the park, of which Crystal Cave is largest, are of interest. The outstanding feature of Sequoia is the Giant Forest. The towering red columns of the sequoia trunks, rising clean among the huge white firs, incense cedars, sugar and ponderosa pines, and disappearing amid the foliage of these smaller trees, amaze the visitor. He may spend days wandering through this marvelous forest, finding sequoias singly and in groups, in hundreds, thousands, even in many thousands if he counts the seedlings; yet he never outlives his first surprise. Here he must readjust his sense of proportion. Those who spend years in the reservation say that they never cease to marvel at the majesty of the trees. Adding to the beauty of the sequoia forest are numerous small, flower-filled meadows where bordering sequoias retain their limbs and foliage far down along their trunks. The estimated age of the oldest sequoias approximates 4000 years, and many of the trees attain a height of 300 feet with trunk diameters of twenty feet. Nuttall's dogwood, western white, whitebark and lodgepole pine also grow in the park.

The Kings Canyon area, adjoining Sequoia on the north, was established in 1940 to preserve its rugged mountains, canyons and sequoia forests in a roadless wilderness. To this park were added the groves of the former General Grant National Park, the latter having been abolished as a separate national park in the same year. Added, also, were 10,000 acres of Redwood Mountain and Redwood Canyon. The Kings Canyon reservation totals an area of 710 square miles. It extends westward from the splintered crest of the Sierra and contains a number of spectacular canyons including Tehipite Valley, one of the most striking features in American scenery. Wholly lacking the Yosemite Valley type of beauty, it is larger, more rugged, and its walls higher. Tehipite Dome, rising from the north wall, is 3200 feet above the valley floor, and is one of the five greatest rocks of the scenic world, the others being El Capitan and Half Dome in Yosemite, Grand Sentinel in Kings River Canyon, and the Great White Throne in Zion National Primeval Park. Opposite Tehipite Dome rises Mount Harrington from whose summit cascades tumble into the Middle Fork of the Kings River.

Besides the upper watersheds of the Middle and South forks of the Kings, the park includes Evolution Valley and the famous Evolution basin at the headwaters of the South Fork of the San Joaquin River. It is regrettable, but important to note, that

The sequoia trees are the oldest living things in the world. Through the efforts of a few far-sighted men during the latter part of the nineteenth century, the Giant Forest in Sequoia Park was saved from ax, saw, and dynamite for the enjoyment of Americans for all time.

In the scene above, a group of riders heads for the crest of the Sierra Nevada along the High Sierra Trail in Sequoia. Below, the National Park Service conducts a campfire program at Giant Forest in Sequoia. Popular with visitors are the informal singing and the illustrated talks by ranger naturalists at these programs held in the evening throughout the National Park System.

In the warm glow of late afternoon light, Castle
Rocks are seen across Kaweah Canyon from the High
Sierra Trail in Sequoia. The tree is a ponderosa pine.

[69]

Throughout most of its range within the United States the bighorn sheep is declining in numbers. In Glacier, Yellowstone, Rocky Mountain, Sequoia-Kings Canyon, Zion and Grand Teton it finds protection from gunners.

the magnificent climax portions of the canyons of the Middle and South forks—in a compromise with power and irrigation interests—were omitted from the park at the time of establishment. These were left available as the Cedar Grove and Tehipite reclamation withdrawals for possible future commercial utilization as reservoir sites. If public opinion fails to prevent such development, these two superb canyons may be flooded and lost forever to future generations as was the Hetch Hetchy Valley in Yosemite National Primeval Park.

Mammals inhabiting the Sequoia-Kings Canyon National Primeval Park include black bear and mule deer which are numerous, the latter wandering unafraid about the campgrounds. Other mammals in the park are marmot, coyote, cony, gray fox, Columbia gray and Douglas squirrels, mountain beaver, porcupine, badger, ringtail, opossum, raccoon, marten, and in the high rocky peaks, bighorn sheep. One of the strange plants that inhabits the forests is the flowering fungus scientifically known as *Pleuricospora fimbriolata*. A species found in sunny exposed places is the bright red hummingbird trumpet. The meadows bordering the little alpine lakes are veritable wildflower gardens in spring and summer, while the chaparral-covered foothills in the park are fragrant in early spring with the blooms of buckthorn, manzanita, wild lilac and many other trees and shrubs native to this lower elevation.

Headquarters for both areas is at Ash Mountain on the General's Highway, with the post office address Sequoia National Park, California. In Sequoia, accommodations are available at Giant Forest Lodge from May to September. Cabins are also available here, as well as housekeeping cabins at Camp Kaweah and at Pinewood Shelter. Hospital Rock Camp is open all year. During the summer, Bearpaw Meadow Camp, with tents and meals, is open to hikers and horseback riders. There are several campgrounds in Sequoia. In Kings Canyon there are two camps with cabins at the General Grant Groves and there is a campground here, as well as at Cedar Grove. Giant Forest Winter Camp, when open, is available from September to May. The parks are reached north from Bakersfield, California, on U. S. Highway 99 to the junction with State Route

Padilla Studio, courtesy The Wilderness Society

Zumwalt Meadow in the canyon of the South Fork of
the Kings River, Kings Canyon National Primeval Park, is
one of the spectacular scenic spots in the Sierra Nevada.

This view shows Kearsarge Pinnacles and Kearsarge Lakes in the rugged wilderness of the high Sierra country of Kings Canyon National Primeval Park. These splintered peaks stand opposite Kearsarge Pass, which plunges over the east face of the stupendous Sierra fault block into Owens Valley. The scene below shows the east face of the Sierra Nevada from the valley. The crest of the range forms the eastern boundary of the park.

198 which passes through Visalia to the Ash Mountain entrance of Sequoia, and over State Route 180 from Fresno on U. S. Highway 99 to the General Grant Grove entrance. The Southern Pacific and Santa Fe railroads leave visitors at Fresno and Visalia. Buses of the Pacific Greyhound and Santa Fe Trail System serve these towns. From here there is scheduled bus service to the parks in summer, and on call in winter. The parks are open all year.

SHENANDOAH NATIONAL PARK, an area of 302 square miles, established in 1935, is in the Blue Ridge Mountains of Virginia. The park, eighty miles west of Washington, D. C., is seventy-five miles in length, and extends from the town of Front Royal on the north to Jarman Gap on the south. The highest point in the park is Hawksbill Mountain 4049 feet above sea level. The Skyline Drive winds along the ridge through the whole length of the park, and affords wide views of the valleys and distant ranges to east and west. The Appalachian Trail, which runs from Maine to Georgia, also follows the ridge, and is joined by numerous others that form a network of trails through the park. Shelters at intervals along the main trail provide overnight sleeping accommodations for hikers. Hemlock and pine are scattered through the park's forests, which are chiefly of hardwoods that make a display of color in autumn. Large white trillium, pink azalea and mountain laurel, make conspicuous floral shows in spring, and these together with pink lady's slipper, bloodroot, hepatica, marigold, golden groundsel, turk's cap lily, wood lily and closed gentian are among the important flowering species of the park. Gray and red fox, raccoon, bobcat, Virginia white-tailed deer, opossum, gray and flying squirrels, woodchuck and chipmunk are a few members of the reservation's mammalian population.

Headquarters is five miles east of Luray, Virginia, on U. S. Highway 211. The address is Luray, Virginia. Accommodations from April to about the first of November are available at Big Meadows Lodge, while cabins at Dickey Ridge, Skyland, Big Meadows

Deciduous forests cover the slopes of the Blue Ridge Mountains of Shenandoah National Park. Far below to the west outside the park, is seen the agricultural Shenandoah Valley.

National Park Service

[73]

Devereux Butcher

In spring, Shenandoah's forests are gay with the white blossoms of flowering dogwood trees and the white or pinkish flowers of mountain laurel. The dogwood grows also in Great Smoky Mountains and Mammoth Cave national parks. Mountain laurel, an evergreen shrub with broad, shiny leaves, is native to these same parks where it is decorative in winter. Laurel, as well as the native holly, rhododendron and other evergreens need the protection given them in the parks, for elsewhere in eastern forests they are being mutilated or destroyed for their green at Christmas time, and throughout the year by men supplying florist shops.

Devereux Butcher

Maidenhair spleenwort, a fern of eastern parks, is one of the most delicately beautiful of its kind. Blooming from May to June, the showy orchis with its pink and white flowers, is a native of Shenandoah and other parks in the East. Outside the parks it is becoming rare.

and Swift Run Gap are also available. Restaurants are operated at all of these locations, as well as at Elk Wallow and Panorama. There is a camp ground at Big Meadows, and picnic grounds are located at Big Meadows, Dickey Ridge, Elk Wallow, Lewis Mountain, Pinnacles and South River. For reservations, address the Virginia Sky-Line Company, Inc., Luray, Virginia. The park is reached by road from Winchester and Front Royal, Virginia, on U. S. Highway 522 and State Route 12 going south. U. S. Highway 211 crosses the park at Thornton Gap; U. S. Highway 33 crosses at Swift Run Gap, and U. S. Highway 250 from Charlottesville to Waynesboro, Virginia, connects with the Skyline Drive eight miles below the south end of the park.

WIND CAVE NATIONAL PARK, in South Dakota's Black Hills, was established in 1903 to protect a cave of which ten miles, so far, have been explored. Discovered in 1881, this cave contains limestone formations known as boxwork. This boxwork, which differs greatly from the stalagmite and stalactite formations seen in many large caves, occurs only in the Black Hills, and in appreciable quantities only in this cave. The name of the cave was suggested by the current of wind that flows through it—outward when the barometer is falling, and inward when rising. The park's above-ground area comprises forty-four square miles of rolling prairies and wooded hills used as a preserve for bison, antelope, elk and deer. It was in an effort to save these species, particularly the bison and antelope, from extinction, that the American Bison Society placed breeding stocks of the animals on the reservation in 1912. Other mammals inhabiting the park are the prairie dog, raccoon and coyote. Among the birds there are the prairie sharptailed grouse, red-shafted flicker, mourning dove, red-headed woodpecker, Say's phoebe and horned lark. Ponderosa pine, a dominant tree of the park, grows here with Rocky Mountain cedar; while such deciduous trees as American elm, wild plum, white ash, cottonwood and quaking aspen grow in the valleys. Some of the more common flowering plants are the coneflower, Indian paintbrush, bedstraw, false indigo and columbine.

Headquarters is within the preserve, and the address is Hot Springs, South Dakota. There is a campground with lunchroom and store open from June through August, located near headquarters. Hotel accommodations are available at Hot Springs, ten miles south on U. S. Highway 85A. The park is reached by road south from Custer, South Dakota, or north from Hot Springs on this route. Visitors leave the Chicago, Burlington and Quincy Railroad, or the Chicago and Northwestern Railroad at Hot Springs, Buffalo Gap or Pringle, South Dakota, from which points bus service is available to the park. The park is open all year.

YELLOWSTONE NATIONAL PARK, in northwestern Wyoming, was the first national park. It was established in 1872, after the Washburn Expedition of 1870 had been sent out to verify the reports on the natural wonders of the area. It was while the expedition was in the field that the national park idea was developed. Having explored the region and discovered the geyser basins, the Canyon of the Yellowstone River with its falls, the hot springs and other natural phenomena, members of the expedition, encamped one night at the junction of the Gibbon and Firehole rivers, discussed what they thought should be done to preserve these wonders. The opinion was expressed that members of the party should pre-empt claims surrounding the points of interest for the sake of the profit that might be made from tourists. However, one member, Cornelius Hedges, did not approve of this plan. He suggested that there be no private ownership of any portion of that region, but that the whole of it be set apart as a great national park and that each member of the party make an effort to achieve this goal. N. P. Langford, in his diary of the expedition, says, "His (Hedges) suggestion met with an instantaneous and favorable response from all—except one—of the members of our party, and each hour since the matter was first broached, our enthusiasm has increased. . . . Our purpose to create a park can only be accomplished by untiring work and concerted action in a warfare against the incredulity and unbelief of our national legislators when our proposal shall be presented for their approval. Nevertheless, I believe we can win the battle." Thus, two years later, the Yellowstone National Primeval Park came into being, and today 3472 square miles of primeval wilderness are preserved for the enjoyment and benefit of future generations.

In addition to the features named above, this park is perhaps the nation's outstanding wildlife sanctuary. Hunters and trappers had wrought considerable havoc among the mammals and birds there, prior to park establishment. Furthermore, since the study of wildlife ecology (response to environmental influences) was little understood in those days by park administrators, there resulted much needless persecution of the so-called predator species; and it was not until passage of the Congressional Act of 1894 to protect the birds and animals of the park, that Yellowstone wildlife was saved from the relentless war waged upon it by man. However, the native birds and animals have now been largely restored. During recent years, the practice of artificially feeding bears and bison has been abandoned in an effort to return them to natural conditions. This has been done in accordance with the national policy of exhibiting in the parks all forms of nature as nearly free as possible from interference by man. Today, while driving along the roads, visitors can see moose, black bear, bison, pronghorn antelope, bighorn sheep, elk, coyote and mule deer; and for those willing to walk or ride horseback along the trails through the wilderness portions of the park, grizzly bear also may be seen, besides numerous smaller mammals. There are more than 200 species of birds native to the park, among them the white pelican, a colony of which lives on an island in Yellowstone Lake. Attempts have been made in the past by commercial interests to dam the outlet of the lake. Public opinion has been strong enough to prevent this desecration, but it should be realized that if the level of the lake is raised by damming, it will mean not only the loss of the pelican colony, one of the last in the country, but also the inundation of the natural land and wildlife habitat bordering the lake.

This photograph, taken in 1871 by the late William Henry Jackson, early photographer of national parks, shows the Geological Survey's Hayden Expedition, one of the two expeditions sent into the Yellowstone country to discover what truth, if any, lay in tales of the region told by explore's. Jackson's photographs of the scenery and natural phenomena of the area helped to convince Congress that the Yellowstone country should be made a national park.

Old Faithful in Yellowstone, as well as all features in this and other national parks, belong to everyone. According to the famous Langford diary, Cornelius Hedges was the first to conceive this idea of public ownership. (See page 76)

At Mammoth Hot Springs in Yellowstone National Primeval Park, the water carries limestone in solution. As the water cools, it deposits this to form the terraces that characterize these springs.

The rarest bird in the park is the large white trumpeter swan. This bird, the largest migratory species in North America, had been brought to the verge of extinction by gunners, and the discovery that some still bred in Yellowstone Lake was a surprise to conservationists. Every effort is now being made to hold a permanent breeding stock in the park. During migrations, geese and ducks of many species come to the park's lakes, and those that survive the ordeal of autumn gunning, find here a haven of peace on their long journey southward.

Large expanses of the park consist of grassy meadows, while other areas are covered with the fragrant gray sage. The forests are composed of solid stands of lodgepole pine; while Douglas fir, Engelmann spruce, Rocky Mountain juniper, limber pine, quaking aspen and cottonwood are present, as well as alpine fir and whitebark pine at high elevations. Most interesting among the dozens of flowering plants are the deep blue Rocky Mountain fringed or feather gentian, the yellow glacierlily, the yellow fritillary, which is a small orange or yellow bell tinged with purple, the pale pink calypso inhabiting moist or boggy woodlands, coralroot, Rocky Mountain iris, bitterroot, a small plant with a large pink or white flower, and the pinkish purple shooting star.

Yellowstone Park headquarters is at Mammoth Hot Springs within the park near the north entrance, and the address is Yellowstone Park, Wyoming. Accommodations are available at Mammoth Hot Springs Hotel, Canyon Hotel, Lake Hotel beside Yellowstone Lake, and at Old Faithful Inn near the famous Old Faithful Geyser. Lodges are maintained at Mammoth Hot Springs near park headquarters, Canyon, Old Faithful, Yellowstone Lake and at Camp Roosevelt near Tower Falls. Cabins are for rent at Mammoth Hot Springs, Canyon, Old Faithful, Fishing Bridge, West Thumb and at Camp Roosevelt. Many campgrounds are also available to visitors who bring their own equipment. The park is reached over the following highways: U. S. Highway 89 from Livingston, Montana, to the Gardiner entrance on the north; U. S. Highway 12 from Billings, Montana, to the Silver Gate entrance at the northeast corner of the park;

George A Grant

Impressive features of Yellowstone Park are the canyon of the
Yellowstone River and the Lower Fall with its tremendous thunder.
The bison inhabits both Yellowstone and Wind Cave National Parks.

I. C. Allen

U. S. Highway 20 from Cody, Wyoming, to the Sylvan Pass entrance on the east; U. S. Highway 89 from Jackson, Wyoming, and U. S. Highway 287 from Rawlins, Wyoming, to the south entrance; and U. S. Highway 191 from Idaho Falls, Idaho, to the West Yellowstone entrance on the west. From Bozeman, Montana, U. S. Highway 191 also goes to West Yellowstone. Railroads serving the park are as follows: The Northern Pacific from Livingston to Gardiner, Montana, and from Laurel to Red Lodge, Montana; the Union Pacific to West Yellowstone and to the south entrance via the Jackson Hole country from Victor, Idaho; the Chicago, Burlington and Quincy to Cody, Wyoming; and the Chicago, Milwaukee, St. Paul and Pacific to the Gallatin Gateway. From these points the Yellowstone Park Transportation Company buses operate into the park. The park is open from June 20 to September 12, although some accommodations are available when the roads are free of snow about May 15 to October 15.

YOSEMITE NATIONAL PARK was established by Act of Congress in the year 1890. However, the famous Yosemite Valley and the Mariposa Grove of sequoia trees were set aside in 1864 to be administered by the State of California. The primeval park comprises 1189 square miles of glacier-sculptured valleys and summits of the Sierra Nevada of California. Yosemite Valley itself affords one of the most awe-inspiring sights anywhere in the National Park System. Countless centuries of glacial action has worn the gray walls of the valley into domes and spires that in some places rise more than 4000 feet above the valley floor. A few of these towering rock formations are the Cathedral Spires, Basket Dome, Half Dome, North Dome, Sentinel Dome and El Capitan. Over the valley walls, like slender white plumes, plunge some of the world's highest and most beautiful waterfalls. Best known of these are the Vernal, Illilouette, Nevada, Bridalveil, Ribbon, which is the highest, 1612 feet, and Upper Yosemite, the second highest free-leaping fall in the world, having a drop of 1430 feet. Among the many peaks along the Sierra crest east of the Yosemite Valley, Mount Lyell is the highest, 13,095 feet above sea level. Although most visitors see the park in summer, increasing numbers of people are visiting it in winter, for it is then that the park takes on a new beauty. Storms cloak the forest and domes in snow, drifting clouds wreathe the summits,

Glacier-carved Half Dome provides a background for the mule deer grazing in the meadows of Yosemite Valley in Yosemite National Primeval Park.

Ralph Anderson

Above is a view of Yosemite Valley from the west, showing El Capitan at left and Bridalveil Fall. One of the beauties of Yosemite is the plunging, swaying drapery of Yosemite Falls (opposite). The upper fall, having a drop of 1430 feet, is the second highest free leaping fall in the world.

and sometimes when the snow is whipped by gales along the high Sierra crest, snow banners can be seen weaving off into the sky, glittering against the blue.

Tree life in the park ranges from chaparral species like manzanita and buckthorn, with live oak and Digger pine on the hot, dry lower slopes, to mountain hemlock and whitebark pine in the alpine country. In the intermediate zones are black oak, incense cedar, ponderosa, Jeffrey and sugar pine, red, white and Douglas fir and sequoia. Of the latter there are three groves in the park. In the Mariposa Grove there are as many as 200 trees with trunks ten feet or more in diameter at breast height. The Grizzly Giant is the largest sequoia in the park, having a trunk diameter of twenty-seven and a half feet, a circumference of ninety-six feet and a height of 209 feet. Its age is estimated to be 3800 years. Mammals of Yosemite include black bear, mule deer, marten, coyote, gray fox, yellow-bellied marmot, Douglas squirrel, cony and porcupine. The blue-fronted Steller jay is abundant in the valleys, and the water ouzel is frequently met with in the canyons.

The classic example of commercial invasion and desecration, within the National Park System, took place in Yosemite National Primeval Park. A water supply dam, authorized by Congress in 1913 and begun in 1922, now floods the park's Hetch Hetchy Valley. This valley was second in scenic beauty only to Yosemite Valley itself, but it has been lost to the nation because the expression of public opposition was not sufficiently strong to outweigh the demands of the small group.

Headquarters of Yosemite is within the park, and the address is Yosemite National Park, California. Hotels that are open all year are the Ahwahnee and the Yosemite Lodge with housekeeping cabins. Accommodations are also available from May or June

Hetch Hetchy Valley, once a wilderness beauty spot in Yosemite National Primeval Park, is today submerged beneath an artificial lake with fluctuating water levels and unsightly shore lines. Dam construction, forced by water supply and hydroelectric power interests early in this century, was bitterly fought by those who valued untouched landscapes, and who realized the danger, through precedent, to all other national parks, if a dam were built. The struggle was lost, and the natural beauty of the valley, too, was lost to the nation forever.

Martin Litton

In the quiet of early morning a mule deer wanders
among the ancient oaks of Yosemite Valley.

to September at Camp Curry, Glacier Point Hotel, Wawona Hotel, and Big Trees Lodge, and from July to September, at Tuolumne Meadows Lodge on the Tioga Pass road.

Along the High Sierra Trail there are five hikers' camps situated about ten miles apart. There are also four campgrounds in the park. Yosemite is reached from the west on State Route 140 from Merced and State Route 41 from Fresno, and from Stockton and Modesto by way of the Big Oak Flat road. From the east, Tioga Pass road to the park, open from late June until mid-October, joins U. S. Highway 395 near Mono Lake. Buses to Merced all year and to Fresno in summer connect with Yosemite Tansportation System buses for the park. During the summer there is bus service also from Lake Tahoe via Tioga Pass. The park is open all year.

Devereux Butcher for National Parks Magazine

Not to be counted among the beauties and wonders of Yosemite Valley are two tile swimming pools which intrude upon the valley's natural scene; or the stage from which raucous jazz blares nightly during summer. National primeval parks are not resorts, and such developments are inconsistent with the purposes of the parks.

Devereux Butcher for National Parks Magazine

Glacier Point Lookout, overlooking Yosemite Valley and the surrounding high country, contains an exhibit explaining the glacial origin of the valley. The exhibit, graphic and interesting, is typical of others in the national parks and monuments provided to help visitors understand the great spectacles of nature. Cross country skiing in Yosemite and certain other national parks attracts more people every year. It is one of the important uses of the reservations, for it makes possible the enjoyment of the winter wilderness. Unsuited to national parks are ski resorts with their parking lots, buildings and ski lifts for the attraction of crowds. To prevent destruction of the wilderness character of the primeval parks, establishment of such developments within these parks must continue to be resisted vigorously.

Ranger naturalists of the National Park Service conduct daily walks to interpret nature for young and old. Wild flowers, trees, birds, mammals and geologic formations are observed and discussed, and visitors' questions are answered. Here a naturalist explains Yosemite Valley's wonders to a group of youngsters.

ZION NATIONAL PARK, located in alluring southern Utah, was established in 1919 to protect 148 square miles of spectacular canyon country. Zion Canyon, about fifteen miles long, was carved by the Virgin River which flows through the park. The soft, cool greens of cottonwood, boxelder and willow along the river on the canyon floor offer a pleasing contrast to the dark red coloring of the surrounding canyon walls. Over the upper slopes pinyon pine and juniper make a deep green blanket. The highest point in the park is West Temple, 7795 feet above sea level and 3802 feet above the canyon floor. The Great White Throne, one of the outstanding rock formations in the park, rises 2394 feet sheer from the floor of the valley. Trails lead to all important parts of the park that are not accessible by road. The windswept highlands are noteworthy for their broad vistas.

Among the park's mammals are such species as gray fox, mule deer, bighorn sheep, mountain lion, coyote, bobcat, porcupine, yellow-bellied marmot and squirrel. Over 150 different varieties of birds have been recorded from the area, including the water ouzel, which inhabits the cool canyons.

Headquarters is within the park, and the address is Springdale, Utah. Zion Lodge and Camp Center housekeeping cabins provide accommodations. There are two public campgrounds. State Route 15 runs through the park. This connects on the west with U. S. Highway 91 from Cedar City or St. George, and on the east wth U. S. Highway 89 from Kanab or Mt. Carmel. The Union Pacific Railroad leaves visitors at Cedar City,

Union Pacific Railroad, courtesy Nature Magazine

From high on the rim, nearly the full length of Zion Canyon can be seen. The Great White Throne is at left and the Virgin River and park road wind along the canyon floor. Zion's walls are dark red and orange, in some places grading to almost pure white at the top.

The Great White Throne, massive symbol of Zion,
rises nearly half a mile above the canyon floor.
It is composed of sandstone deposited millions of
years ago when this land formed the bed of a sea.

Behind the delicate greens of willows and cottonwood stands the red shaft of the Temple of Sina-
wava in the upper end of Zion Canyon. Part of
the Great White Throne is visible in the distance.

and the Denver and Rio Grande Western at Marysvale. The Utah Parks Company provides bus service from both points to the park. Zion is open all year.

EVERGLADES NATIONAL PARK (proposed),

located on the southern tip of the Florida peninsula, will comprise a land and water area of 1892 square miles. This is the only place in the United States that is touched by the tropical life zone which here roughly forms a crescent around the tip of the peninsula. The proposed park will differ, therefore, from all other national parks in having a flora with tropical affinities. Within the proposed park's boundaries are broad expanses of sawgrass marsh, hammock lands of dense jungle growth, prairies interspersed with picturesque stands of cabbage palm and moss-draped cypress, and mangrove forests along the coastal margins. In addition to the mainland area, the park will include most of Florida Bay and numerous keys. The most outstanding tree of the Everglades is the royal palm, tallest and most graceful of its kind. It is native to only this one section in all North America. Other interesting trees are the coppery barked gumbo limbo and the strangler fig, the latter a member of the rubber family. The fig, starting its life from a seed lodged in a crevice of bark on another tree, sends roots down and branches up, eventually enveloping and killing the host tree. Saw palmetto, needle palm, live oak and Madiera mahogany also grow in the proposed park area. In the forested parts there are epiphytes or air plants, numerous ferns, epiphytic orchids and other floral species.

The most remarkable feature of the Everglades is its bird life. Nowhere else in the United States are there such large congregations of birds. The rare, pink roseate spoonbill still breeds here in small colonies in Florida Bay. This species is found nesting elsewhere in North America today only on certain islands off the Texas coast. In the Everglades there are two species of ibis, the wood and white, which nest in rookeries. There are seven species of heron—the Ward's, great white, little blue, green, black-crowned night, yellow-crowned night and Louisiana. There are three egrets—the American, snowy and reddish, the latter being still extremely rare.

During the early part of this century the egrets and spoonbills were slaughtered and were nearly exterminated by plume hunters catering to the millinery trade. Public opinion became aroused just in time to save the birds. Laws were enacted prohibiting the killing of wild birds for their plumage, and patrolled sanctuaries were established in the coastal areas of the Everglades region. Today these interesting birds exist again in large numbers to be enjoyed by all who care to see them. Other notable birds of the Everglades are the water turkey or anhinga, chuck-will's-widow, swallow-tailed kite, short-tailed hawk, white-crowned pigeon, several species of ducks, purple and Florida gallinules, bald eagle and turkey. Being in the path of the eastern route of birds that migrate from the West Indies and South America, a large number of the song and insectivorous migrants known to the eastern part of the United States breed or pass through this region. Cougar, black bear, gray and mangrove fox squirrel, raccoon, opossum, otter, gray fox, Florida spotted skunk, manatee or sea cow and white-tailed deer are among the mammals of the proposed park. There are several snakes here as well, and these include the black snake, king snake, tree snake and water moccasin in the swampy areas; while the coral snake and rattlesnake inhabit drier locations. The American crocodile and the alligator exist in small numbers.

In 1945 the proposed park area was established as a federal wildlife refuge to be administered by the U. S. Fish and Wildlife Service. This was done as a means of protecting the area and its wildlife which were rapidly being destroyed by fire and shooting. The warden patrol and bird sanctuaries already established here by the National Audubon Society were thus supplemented by the additional warden patrol of the federal service. Cooperation between the State of Florida and the federal government should bring the park into being before long, unless the recent discovery of oil in the vicinity should lead to the area's being made unsuitable for national park status.

The royal palm grows nowhere in the United States except in the proposed Everglades National Primeval Park. It needs the protection the park would give it.

Allan D. Cruickshank

The snowy egret and other birds of the Everglades were once slaughtered and almost exterminated by plume hunters supplying the millinery trade. Public opinion intervened, and today, because of protective laws and the establishment of sanctuaries, these birds again exist in abundance for the delight of all who want to see them. Watery expanses of the Everglades are grown with sawgrass and are picturesquely dotted with clumps of cabbage palms.

Department of the Interior

The translucent green frond of a young
cabbage palm is a thing of beauty.

The strangler fig, native of the Everglades, starts
life on other trees which it uses for support, finally enveloping them and strangling them to death.

If the Everglades is established as a national park, its native Seminole Indians will be an attraction there. The Seminoles are a conglomerate of several Florida tribes, with an admixture of Negro. During the early part of the nineteenth century, there was the usual conflict between whites and Indians that accompanied settlement in other parts of the country. Attempts by the United States Government to enforce treaties, and an effort to have the Seminoles move out of south Florida, precipitated the Seminole War in 1833. The war ended when it became apparent that, secure in their Everglades retreat, the Seminoles could not be subjugated. The Seminoles travel through the intricate waterways of the 'Glades in dugout canoes of cypress, which they propel with a pole. Characteristic of the Seminoles are the colorful clothing, bright strings of beads and the elaborate hair-do of the squaws.

Devereux Butcher
for National Parks Magazine

NATIONAL NATURE MONUMENTS

ARCHES NATIONAL MONUMENT, situated in southeastern Utah, was established in 1929. It consists of five separate areas totaling fifty-four square miles. The name Arches is derived from the many natural arches formed by water, freezing and thawing, wind-blown sand and other forms of weathering in a 300-foot thick layer of red rock called the Entrada Sandstone. Geologists explain that the Entrada Sandstone has been cut by two series of master joints or cracks intersecting at right angles. These cracks pass through the entire thickness of the formation. For thousands of years, water entering the cracks has dissolved the sandstone, thereby enlarging the joints and leaving fissures between slabs or "fins" of rock that are sometimes less than twenty feet thick, yet more than a hundred feet high. It is in these fins that many of the arches have been formed. Once the fin has been perforated, weathering and the force of gravity enlarge the opening until it becomes an arch. Continued erosion wears it thinner until it falls, leaving remnants standing as buttresses at either end. All stages in the development and decay of such arches may be seen in the monument.

The Windows section, weirdly scenic like the others, reached by a nine-mile drive over an ungraded road that leaves U. S. Highway 160 twelve miles north of Moab, Utah, is the most accessible area in the monument. The main features here are Double Arch, Parade of the Elephants, North and South Windows and Turret Arch. In the Devil's Garden section are huge amphitheaters joined by twisting passageways among rows of gigantic fins in which erosion has cut steeples, towers, spires and arches. Of the eighty-one arches recorded in the monument, more than sixty occur in this section. Landscape Arch, believed to be the longest natural bridge in the world, has a span of 291 feet. The Delicate Arch is reached by a twenty-six mile drive from U. S. Highway 160 down the picturesque Salt Valley and a two mile hike from the end of the road. This arch is beyond description, with its unsurpassed setting of massive "slickrock" and precipitous cliffs. The Klondyke Bluffs section is directly west of the north end of the Devil's Garden and can be reached by a three mile hike. In this section are Tower Arch, Joseph Smith and the Golden Plates. The Courthouse Towers section can be reached by a two-mile walk from monument headquarters. This contains several massive walled canyons, the most spectacular being known as Park Avenue. Desert flowers are an added attraction during May and June with desert mallow, lupine, larkspur, pentstemon, yucca and various species of cacti. The animal life on the desert is sparse because of lack of water, but occasional glimpses may be had of coyote and fox. Deer and mountain lion are present in the upper elevations of the monument, and mountain sheep have been seen.

Headquarters is five miles northwest of Moab, Utah, on U. S. Highway 160, and can be reached from Cortez, Colorado, on the south, or Crescent Junction, on U. S. Highway 50 on the north. Accommodations are not available in the monument, but there are modern cabins and a hotel at Moab. A through bus line runs from Albuquerque, New Mexico, to Salt Lake City, Utah, passing through Moab, and bus service is available from Thompsons, Utah, on the Denver and Rio Grande Western Railroad. Arrangements can be made in Moab for transportation to the monument, which is open all year.

THE ANTIQUITIES ACT (an act for the preservation of American antiquities), passed by Congress in 1906, provides under section 2, "That the President of the United States is hereby authorized, in his discretion, to declare by public proclamation historic landmarks, historic and prehistoric structures, and other objects of historic or scientific interest that are situated upon the lands owned or controlled by the Government of the United States to be national monuments. . . ." Most of the national nature monuments here described were established by Presidential proclamation under authority of this act. The act eliminates delay in placing under federal

Tower Arch is but one of nature's massive architectural structures in Arches National Monument, Utah.

protection objects or areas of national importance that are being, or are about to be, despoiled. A number of areas thus have been saved from pending injury. It was the rapid exploitation of Arizona's petrified forest that influenced passage of the act.

BADLANDS NATIONAL MONUMENT, in southern South Dakota's White River Badlands, was set aside in 1939. It contains 207 square miles of unusually beautiful erosion. A number of the formations are as high as 300 feet, and are composed of layers of clay and sand washed from the Black Hills. They range in color from green, cream and yellow to pink. The erosion continues today with every rain. Bones have been found of such prehistoric animals as the saber-tooth tiger, the three-toed horse, and of ancestors of the rhinoceros, hog and camel that inhabited the swamps once covering this region. Although elk, Audubon bighorn sheep and bison lived here before the surrounding country was settled, these species have been extirpated. A few mule deer, as well as smaller mammals such as chipmunk, ground squirrel, prairie dog, badger, jack and cottontail rabbit, raccoon, skunk, red fox, bobcat and coyote are still to be found. Here also are such wild flowers as ground-phlox, pasque flower, wallflower, evening primrose, yellow pea, red mallow, mariposa lily, purple, blue and white

The grotesquely eroded hills of the Badlands are of multi-colored clay and sand.

Stevens Heckscher

pentstemon, yucca and prickly pear cactus, the latter bearing blossoms of yellow and red. The principal tree is the Rocky Mountain cedar.

Headquarters is within the monument at Cedar Pass. Meals and cabins are provided at Cedar Pass Lodge, and lunches and supplies are obtainable at Pinnacles during the summer. Emergency gas, meals, and lodging can be obtained at Cedar Pass throughout the year. The monument is reached from the east over U. S. Highway 16 from Sioux Falls, South Dakota, to the junction with State Route 40 seven miles west of Kadoka, South Dakota. It is reached from the west also over U. S. Highway 16 from Rapid City, South Dakota, to Wall, where a road branches south six miles to the monument. The Chicago, Milwaukee, St. Paul and Pacific, and the Chicago and Northwestern railroads serve Rapid City. From June 1 to September 1 the Black Hills Transportation Company runs daily busses from Rapid City to the Badlands. The monument is open all year.

BLACK CANYON OF THE GUNNISON NATIONAL MONUMENT, established in 1933, covers twenty-two square miles in western Colorado. It embraces the deepest and most spectacular ten-mile section of the dark, formidable gorge of the Gunnison River. Ute Indians aptly describe this gorge—a distance of approximately fifty miles between Sapinero and Austin—as "the place of high rocks and much water." Geologists consider the Black Canyon of the Gunnison River as probably the most remarkable bit of scenery in the entire San Juan Mountain region. For several hundred million years the Gunnison River has been furiously carving its channel through the pre-Cambrian complex, the oldest matter in geologic history. The hills surrounding and rising above the canyon rims are of so much more recent origin than the rocks of the gorge itself that, during the gap of time thus represented, life developed from the single plant cell to the dinosaur. The rims of the gorge are only 1300 feet apart at the closest point, yet the gorge ranges from 1730 feet to 2425 feet in depth within the monument. At one location the river channel narrows to forty feet. In addition to this stupendous and spectacular gorge, the areas bordering both rims of the monument have unusual natural beauty. Dense scrub oak, juniper and some of the oldest pinyons (550 to 750 years old) known to tree-ring scientists cover the summit area, with Douglas fir growing in the canyon. Flowering shrubs such as serviceberry, mock orange and mountain mahogany are common. The monument is one of the last strongholds of the Rocky Mountain bighorn sheep, while the Rocky Mountain mule deer,

[100]

The Black Canyon of the Gunnison River, averaging 2078 feet in depth and only 1300 feet in width at the narrowest point, has required several million years for its formation. The rock of this gorge, according to geologists, is the oldest matter in geologic history. Rocky Mountain bighorn sheep inhabit the monument.

elk, bear, mink, yellow-bellied marmot, badger and porcupine are found in abundance.

The monument is under the supervision of Mesa Verde National Park, and the address is Mesa Verde National Park, Colorado. Both rims of the monument are accessible by automobile during good summer weather. From Montrose, Colorado, the distance to the south rim is eight miles via U. S. Highway 50, and nine miles north over a graded road. The north rim is reached from State Route 92 just east of Crawford. There is no bus service to the reservation. A campground is maintained on each rim, and a park ranger is stationed there during the travel season. Supplies are not obtainable at the monument. Hotel and tourist-camp facilities are available in Montrose.

CAPITOL REEF NATIONAL MONUMENT, in south central Utah, established in 1937, comprises an area of fifty-one square miles. Situated in rugged desert country, the chief feature of the area is a buttressed cliff of highly colored sandstone that derives its name from white sandstone domes resting upon lower strata. Geologists say that the cliff is one of the finest known examples of what is termed a water pocket fold or monocline, which is the result of an upheaval of the earth's crust. This action

The chief feature at Capitol Reef is a colorful sandstone cliff.

National Park Service

Capulin Mountain, an extinct volcano in New
Mexico, is believed by geologists to have last
erupted as recently as two thousand years ago.

is believed to have taken place several million years ago. Erosion has exposed the upturned layers of strata.

The area is administered by the superintendent of Zion National Primeval Park, and the address is Springdale, Utah. Its southern boundary lies along State Route 24 running south a hundred miles from U. S. Highway 50 at Green River, Utah, and east eighty-four miles from U. S. Highway 89 at Sigurd, Utah. There are no accommodations at the monument. Fruita, on State Route 24, is the nearest town. The monument is open all year.

CAPULIN MOUNTAIN NATIONAL MONUMENT, in northern New Mexico, established in 1916, comprises an area of about a square mile. The monument protects the large volcanic cinder cone for which the area is named, which rises 8215 feet above sea level, 1500 feet above the surrounding plain, and has a rim diameter of 1450 feet. The reservation is located in a large area of volcanic remains. Geologically this cone is of recent origin. According to geologists, it last erupted approximately two thousand years ago. From the rim, one can see in every direction the lava beds that flowed from the crater like molasses, forming waves and folds as they flowed over each other seeking lower levels. Unfortunately, the symmetry of the cone has been marred by a road to the summit. The road is visible from all points. Two major foot trails have been constructed, one around the rim on the crest, a distance of one mile, and the other from the end of the road to the bottom of the crater 400 feet below.

Headquarters is at the town of Capulin, New Mexico, three miles south of the monument. There are no accommodations for visitors, except at nearby towns. The monument is reached over U. S. Highway 64 from Capulin on the south, and from Raton, New Mexico, on the west over U. S. Highway 87, a distance of twenty-nine miles. Eight Greyhound busses pass through Capulin daily, four each way. Cars may be hired at Capulin, and between busses one may make the trip, which requires about two hours. The monument is open all year.

CEDAR BREAKS NATIONAL MONUMENT, in southern Utah, was established in 1933. Comprising an area of nine square miles, its chief feature is an amphitheater of eroded sandstone and limestone, the dominant color of which is bright orange-pink. Though having the same geological formation as Bryce Canyon National Primeval Park, it is more varied in color, but lacks the innumerable delicately carved spires of Bryce. The highest point of the amphitheater rim is 2000 feet above the lowest point

Cedar Breaks, high in southern Utah's Markagunt Plateau, is an amphitheater of brightly
colored eroded sandstone and limestone.

in the eroded canyons below. Surrounded by the Dixie National Forest, it is located at an altitude of 10,400 feet above sea level on the Markagunt Plateau. It is a magnificent bit of mountain country where trees such as bristlecone or foxtail pine, white and alpine fir, Engelmann spruce and golden aspen are found. Among the many wild flowers of the area are larkspur, lupine and white columbine.

The monument is administered jointly with Zion National Primeval Park, and the address is Springdale, Utah. Cedar Breaks Lodge and cabins are open for visitors from June 1 to September 20. A campground is available to those who bring their own equipment. The monument is reached on State Route 14 east from U. S. Highway 91 at Cedar City, Utah, and west from U. S. Highway 89 which connects with State Route 14 twenty-four miles north of the Mt. Carmel Highway to Zion National Primeval Park. The Union Pacific Railroad leaves visitors at Cedar City, and from here the busses of the Utah Parks Company conduct tours to the monument en route to Zion and Bryce Canyon national primeval parks. The monument is open from about June 1 to November 1, depending on weather conditions.

CHANNEL ISLANDS NATIONAL MONUMENT, established in 1938, consists of Santa Barbara and Anacapa islands off the coast of Southern California, with a combined area of a little more than one and a half square miles. Sealions come to the island's beaches in large numbers, and there is an abundance of bird and plant life. Fossils have been found, including those of Pleistocene elephants. The islands, under joint administration with Sequoia National Primeval Park, California, have not yet been developed for visitors, and there is, therefore, no established boat service to them. Yachting parties sometimes stop there from the nearest mainland points which are Hueneme, San Pedro and other ports near Los Angeles.

CHIRICAHUA NATIONAL MONUMENT, in southern Arizona, was established in 1924 to protect sixteen square miles of brown and gray rhyolite monoliths that have eroded into weird shapes. Rhyolite is an acid volcanic rock, the lava form of granite. By these formations, which belong to the Tertiary Period, the geologic history of millions of years is told. Geologists say that once the area was full of volcanic activity, and that molten basalt and rhyolite poured out over the level land. As the lava cooled, it shrank and cracked in patterns. Then, after all volcanic activity had ended, the heaving of the earth's crust tilted and lifted the cracked lava into mountains. This was followed by countless centuries of erosion, which formed the strange landscape of today with its monoliths, balancing rocks and canyons.

Besides the geologic exhibit, there is much plant and animal life. Chiricahua is a mountain range rising from an arid grassland, with rain and winter snows providing moisture for vegetation and wildlife. The deep canyons and cool north slopes are clothed in green, while the dry southward facing slopes have plant life characteristic of the desert. There are several species of pine, two of juniper, Arizona cypress, madrone and six species of oak, manzanita, and among the plants there are several cacti, yucca, scarlet pentstemon, bovardia and century plant. Arizona white-tail deer are abundant, as well as numerous smaller mammals. Among the birds are the coppery-tailed trogon and the thick-billed parrot which sometimes come to the area from Mexico. Present also is the band-tailed pigeon, now becoming rare throughout its wide range because of killing by gunners.

Headquarters is within the monument, and the address is Dos Cabezos, Arizona. The Silver Spur Ranch at Dos Cabezos, a quarter mile from headquarters, provides accommodations for visitors, while free campgrounds are maintained in the monument for those who bring their own equipment. Saddle horses are available. Chiricahua is reached east from Tucson over U. S. Highway 80 to Benson, Arizona, and thence over State Route 86 and U. S. Highway 666 to Willcox, Arizona, where a branch road leads thirty-six miles southeast to the monument. The reservation is open all year.

The geologic history of many million years is told by Chiricahua's
brown and gray rhyolite monoliths of the Tertiary Period.

COLORADO NATIONAL MONUMENT, established in 1911, is situated in west
central Colorado. It consists of twenty-eight square miles of canyons with walls of
eroded red sandstone carved by water and wind. The geologic origin of the sandstone,

The red sandstone cliffs and columns of Colorado National Monument make
this reservation highly scenic, attracting large numbers of visitors each year.

the shales and the layer of black granite in the canyon walls tell a story covering millions of years of earth building. Monoliths and cliffs a thousand feet high make the monument one of outstanding scenic beauty. A highway winds for twenty-two miles along the canyon rims, providing spectacular views. Among the mammals of Colorado National Monument there are bison, elk, gray fox, coyote and mule deer. Because the country is semi-arid, there are no tall forests, but on the escarpments there are stands of pinyon pine and juniper. In spring there are wild flowers in the canyons and on the tablelands.

The monument is under the direct supervision of the Superintendent of Mesa Verde National Park, who is represented at the monument by a year-round resident custodian in charge. The address is Fruita, Colorado. There is a free campground on the reservation, and other accommodations are available at nearby towns. The eastern entrance to the monument is four miles from Grand Junction, Colorado, located on U. S. highways 6, 24, and 50, and the northern entrance three and a half miles from Fruita on U. S. highways 6 and 50, making the monument easily accessible to transcontinental travel. It is open all year.

CRATERS OF THE MOON NATIONAL MONUMENT, in southern Idaho, was established in 1924. There is no other area so small in size where as many volcanic features can be seen. It consists of seventy-four square miles of craters, cinder cones, lava flows, caves, tunnels formed by lava flowing under a hard crust, and other phenomena that make the area resemble the moon's surface as seen through a telescope. In the caves and tunnels there are red and blue stalagmites and stalactites. Most of the area is without vegetation except for lichens. On some of the lava flows there are a few small pines, shrubs, grass and flowering plants. The area is noted for its weird and unearthly appearance, as well as for its geological interest.

Headquarters is at Arco, Idaho. The monument is reached over U. S. Highway 20 west from Idaho Falls, a distance of 107 miles, and east from Boise over the same route, a distance of 187 miles. For those who bring their own equipment, there is a campground at the monument. Cabins are also available. The monument is open during the summer months.

Craters of the Moon National Monument is well named, for this weird volcanic landscape with its cinder cones and lava flows, resembles the moon's surface as seen through a telescope.

National Park Service

In the foreground is the fantastic erosion at
Zabriski Point, Death Valley National Monument,
and in the distance is Death Valley itself.

Ubehebe Crater, a colorful volcanic cone measuring half a mile across and nearly 800 feet deep, is one of the many amazing features for the protection of which Death Valley was established as a national monument.

DEATH VALLEY NATIONAL MONUMENT, in eastern California and southwestern Nevada, was established in 1933. Comprising an area of 2981 square miles of desert country, it is the fifth largest area under National Park Service administration. From north to south the monument extends 140 miles. Lying between barren, splintered mountain ranges, the Amargosa Range on the east and the Panamints on the west, it is an unspoiled landscape rich in esthetic appeal and scientific interest. The geologic formations, varying from salt flats to volcanic craters and jagged peaks, range in color from white through reds and earth colors to nearly black, which, when touched by the desert sunsets, turn to blazing orange, red and purple contrasted with shadows of brilliant blue. On infrequent days of atmospheric haze the colors are softened to pastel shades that fade in the distance to blend with the sky. The lowest point in the United States is in the valley. This spot, near Badwater, is about 280 feet below sea level. Fifteen miles west of Badwater on the skyline of the Panamints rises Telescope Peak, the highest point in the monument, 11,325 feet above the lowest point. In winter, snow caps the Panamint ridge, while in the valley, from late October to May, the climate is mild. In early times, Death Valley won fame for its summer heat, and this fact is shown by its name. Explorers and travelers, caught here without water, perished in the heat. The highest temperature recorded is 137° in the shade.

Some of the important points of interest within the monument are Dantes View, the crest of the Panamints, Titus Canyon, Ubehebe Crater, Chloride Cliffs, Sand Dunes, Mosaic Canyon and Badwater. Geologists believe that the valley was formed by fracturing and folding of the earth's surface. A geologic study of the area, as yet incomplete, should reveal more important facts about its formation. Fossilized footprints of prehistoric species of carnivores, camels, horses, antelopes and wading birds have been found in the Salt Creek Hills.

There is an abundance of present-day mammals including jack rabbit, badger, gray and kit foxes, coyote, desert bighorn sheep, antelope ground squirrel, wood and kangaroo rats, pocket gophers and pocket mice. Horned toads and lizards, including the large chuckawalla, also inhabit the monument. Among the birds there are the desert raven, roadrunner, Gambel's quail, rock wren, killdeer, western meadowlark, Say's phoebe, and western mourning dove. There are eleven species of cacti including grizzly bear with bright yellow flowers, and beaver tail bearing rose-colored flowers. Other plants are the wetleaf, so named because its leaves are always moist; turtleback, a low-growing plant resembling a turtle and having gray leaves that give off an odor like turpentine; desert trumpet found on alluvial fans and having hollow stems that are expanded below the joints; bear-poppy with white blossoms and blueish leaves covered with long white hairs; several species of desert mariposas, and rocklady, which is found in Titus Canyon and nowhere else in the world. In late winter or early spring, when the season has been sufficiently wet, several plants appear that grow annually from seed. Among them are the curlybloom varying from purple to blue and white, Chinese-lantern with pink globe-shaped flowers, evening and sweet scented golden primroses and desert sunflower. There are eleven species of ferns in the mountains, and these include southern maidenhair and goldfern. Other plant life includes honey mesquite, screwbean, the bright green desert fir which is not a conifer, brittlebush, stingbush, paper-bag bush, desert holly and Death Valley sage. In the mountains at elevations over 5000 feet above sea level, there are western and Utah juniper, Rocky Mountain maple, curlleaf, singleleaf pinyon, limber and bristlecone pines.

Human activity has made history in the valley. Pioneers arrived in the 1850s, and silver miners worked in the surrounding mountains in the 1860s; but the most important, perhaps, was the development of borax mining by two companies beginning in 1884.

Headquarters is within the monument. In winter it is located four miles north of Furnace Creek, and in summer on the Wildrose Canyon road. The address is Death Valley, California. Accommodations are available at Furnace Creek Inn from November 15 to May 1; and at Furnace Creek Auto Camp from September 15 to May 15. Emergency accommodations are available all summer at Stove Pipe Wells Hotel and Scotty's Castle. On the Trona-Death Valley road, near summer headquarters, there are cabins, a restaurant and a store. For those who bring their own equipment, there are several campgrounds. The monument is reached over U. S. Highway 6 north from Los Angeles to Johannesburg where a road branches east to Trona and the monument. From Reno and Carson City, Nevada, it is reached over U. S. Highway 395 south to the junction with U. S. Highway 6 at Bishop, California, and south from there to two miles south of Lone Pine where State Route 190 branches east to the monument. On the east the monument is reached over U. S. Highway 95 north from Las Vegas, Nevada, and south from Tonopah, Nevada, to Beatty, Nevada, at the junction with State Route 58 which leads to the monument. The Union Pacific Railroad leaves visitors at Las Vegas where cars are available. The monument is open from November 1 to May 1.

DEVIL POSTPILE NATIONAL MONUMENT, located in eastern California, is just south of Yosemite National Primeval Park and comprises an area of a little over one square mile. It was established in 1911 to preserve basaltic rock formations of blue-gray hexagonal columns forming a cliff sixty feet high and 300 yards in length. The columns, some vertical, some curving, some radiating from a common center and others slanting, are the result of cooling during a period of volcanic activity. Probably as long ago as 200,000 years, a thousand foot-thick glacier forced itself down the canyon of the Middle Fork of the San Joaquin River where its course was

The Devil Postpile is a cliff of blue-gray basaltic hexagonal columns formed by cooling during volcanic activity.

blocked by the basaltic mass. This the glacier carved away, exposing the columns. Broken pieces of columns form a talus slope at the base of the cliff. One of the beauty spots of the reservation is Rainbow Falls on the San Joaquin River. The monument is in the Sierra Nevada at an elevation of 7600 feet, and is surrounded by the Sierra National Forest.

The area is under the care of the superintendent of Yosemite National Primeval Park. Visitor accommodations are provided at Red Meadows Lodge, just outside the monument boundary. Here also are cabins, a store and a campground. A second campground is situated inside the monument. U. S. Highway 395 south from Reno and Carson City, Nevada, and north from Bishop, California, joins a branch road at Mammoth Lakes, California, which goes to the monument. At present this branch road is narrow, steep and winding, and is in bad condition. The monument is open from July to October.

DEVILS TOWER NATIONAL MONUMENT, in the northeast corner of Wyoming, was established in 1906, the first national monument. Comprising an area of almost two square miles, its chief feature is the 865 foot flat-topped rock called the Devil's Tower. Geologists say that the tower was formed by a stream of molten rock that, in pushing upward, came to a hard layer of the earth's crust and was forced into a dome-shaped mass. In cooling, this mass cracked into vertical columns that eventually were exposed through erosion. The fluted tower is a remnant of the dome. Most of the columns that form the flutings are pentagonal and average ten feet in diameter, while the tower measures 1700 feet in diameter at the base. The color of the rock is light gray and buff, and is partly covered with lichens. The oval top, inhabited by chipmunks and other rodents and birds, comprises one and a half acres, on which grow moss, grass, and sage. Near the top of the sheer sides there are nests of the prairie falcon. A colony of prairie dogs in the monument near the Belle Fourche River attracts the attention of visitors. The tower, which rises from a rolling landscape that is partially covered with a forest predominantly of ponderosa pine, is encircled at its base by a trail.

Headquarters, museum, campground and picnic area are located at the foot of the rock. The address is Devils Tower, Wyoming. There are tourist cabins nearby. The monument is reached over U. S. Highway 14 west from Rapid City, South Dakota,

Rising to a height of 865 feet from a rolling plain, Devils Tower, a huge volcanic
plug, is one of the most extraordinary sights in the National Monument System.

111 miles to a junction with Devils Tower Road. From the west it is reached over
the same highway from Sheridan, Wyoming, 160 miles to the Devils Tower road.
The monument is open all year.

DINOSAUR NATIONAL MONUMENT, located in northeastern Utah and northwestern Colorado, was established in 1915, setting aside eighty acres for the protection

Besides the famous quarry of dinosaur bones, Dinosaur National Monument contains some rugged scenic canyons. This view was taken at the junction of the Yampa and Green rivers. The location is known as Pat's Hole.

of a rich deposit of fossil bones of prehistoric animals. In 1938 the monument was enlarged to 327 square miles to include some of the most spectacular canyon country in the United States. By the slow tilting of the rock masses, the dark sandstone containing the dinosaur fossils was tipped and eroded into view. The dinosaurs inhabited this section of the country approximately 200 million years ago. Scientists believe that this deposit represents a sand bar of an ancient river and that the bodies of dinosaurs, dead from many causes over a period of time, were washed onto the bar by the river. The bones were covered with sand and replaced by the rock-making mineral, silica, becoming in time rocks themselves. This deposit was discovered in 1909 by Dr. Earl Douglass of the Carnegie Museum, Pittsburgh. Twenty-three skeletons have been removed from the quarry by the Carnegie Museum, the Smithsonian Institution, Washington, D. C., and the University of Utah, Salt Lake City. Assembled dinosaur skeletons are on display at these institutions, as well as at the Colorado Museum of Natural History and at several other museums throughout this and other countries. The dinosaur bones within the monument represent twelve species ranging from small ones no larger than a cat, to the mighty brontosaurus or thunder lizard that probably weighed forty tons. One skeleton of the brontosaurus at the Carnegie Museum measures eighty feet in length. The stegosaurus with armor plating, a crest of plates three feet high on its back and yard-long spines on its tail, has been found here, as well as an allosaurus, a fierce, carnivorous dinosaur whose huge jaws were filled with long, sharp teeth having serrated edges like a bread knife. In addition to the dinosaur bones, the fossils of crocodiles, turtles, shells, cycads, leaves and petrified wood have been found.

Although there is not yet an assembled skeleton at Dinosaur National Monument, the National Park Service plans to explore the fossil-bearing layer to uncover specimens which can be exposed in high relief as an exhibit-in-place. Using this as the feature exhibit, a modern museum building is to be constructed over the face of the quarry, and accessory exhibits such as dioramas, mounted and assembled materials, paintings, charts and transparencies will be used for presentation.

Most of the scenic part of the monument, when made accessible, should provide a great deal of interest to visitors. The Yampa River, entering from the east, is a fast flowing stream with rapids, bends and ox-bows, and it has cut an awe-inspiring canyon in places over 1600 feet deep. Entering from the north, the Green River flows through the wild, spectacular canyon of Lodore. A number of Indian caves and rock-shelters are situated in the canyon walls. On the plateaus and mountain slopes of this semi-arid country grow sage, serviceberry, ponderosa pine, Douglas fir, quaking aspen and mountain mahogany. At lower elevations there are shad-scale, greasewood and sage interspersed with pinyon pine and juniper. The canyon bottoms have streambank forests of cottonwood, boxelder, choke-cherry, squawberry and sage, the latter growing taller than a man on horseback. Wild flowers on the reservation include sego lily, desert mallow, sunflower, evening primrose, fritillaria, goldenrod, monkey flower, purple vetch and purple and yellow bee weed. Among the mammals are mule deer, bighorn sheep, black bear, mountain lion, coyote, bobcat, cottontail and jack rabbit, badger, beaver, prairie dog, weasel, bushy-tailed wood rat, and the golden-mantled ground squirrel. Horned toad, several species of lizards and an occasional snake are present. Birds include the golden and bald eagle, most of the larger hawks, western horned owl, sage grouse, a host of smaller birds such as the goldfinch, lazuli bunting, long-tailed chat and chickadee. Canada geese nest on islands in the river.

At Dinosaur National Monument in Utah, the huge
fossil thigh bone of a dinosaur is being lifted from
the quarry which is a veritable prehistoric Noah's Ark.

Carnegie Museum

Fossil Cycad National Monument contains a rich deposit of fossil cycads, plants that grew millions of years ago which resembled tree ferns. This picture shows the flower of a cycadoid accurately restored in glass.

G. R. Wieland,
courtesy The Wilderness Society

Headquarters is within the monument, seven miles north of Jensen, Utah, on U. S. Highway 40. The address is Jensen. There are no accommodations within the reservation, but they are available at Vernal, Utah, twenty-one miles from headquarters west of the monument on U. S. Highway 40. The monument is reached over U. S. Highway 40 west 381 miles from Denver, Colorado, and east 200 miles from Salt Lake City, Utah.

FOSSIL CYCAD NATIONAL MONUMENT, an area of one half square mile located in the southwest corner of South Dakota was established in 1922 as a research national monument because of the remains of fossilized plants, or cycads, embedded there. The plants, which resembled tree ferns, grew millions of years ago during the Mesozoic period when dinosaurs inhabited the earth. As early as 1900, fossil tree trunks were discovered in the monument area, and further investigation brought to light fossilized leaves and buds of the cycad. This monument is not open to the general public, but specimens of the beautiful and delicately formed cycads are on exhibition at Wind Cave National Park and at the National Museum, Washington, D. C. The fossils are not exposed at the monument, but lie underground. Digging is not permitted except by special permission of the National Park Service. The superintendent of Wind Cave has charge of this area, which is situated twenty-five miles southwest of Wind Cave National Park near Minnekahta, South Dakota, and fourteen miles southwest of Hot Springs, South Dakota, just off U. S. Highway 85A.

GLACIER BAY NATIONAL MONUMENT, on the coast of southern Alaska, was established in 1925. An untouched wilderness, it consists of 3590 square miles of snow and ice-capped mountains and arms of the sea. Because of its large receding glaciers, it provides opportunity for study of post-glacial establishment of flora and fauna. At the foot of some of the glaciers the ground rock and lateral moraines are slowly being exposed as the great ice walls melt back a little each year. In places that have been exposed for a time, trees and other vegetation are slowly taking over, while in areas longer exposed, dense forests have become established. Among the important tree species are Sitka spruce, lodgepole pine, black cottonwood, western hemlock, mountain hemlock and alpine fir. The largest glacier is Muir Glacier, named for the naturalist John Muir, who did considerable exploring in the region. The higher peaks are Mount La Perouse, Mount Fairweather, Mount Lituya, Mount Crillon and Mount Quincy Adams. The monument is bordered on the north by the Province of British Columbia and on the south by Icy Strait and Cross Sound. The Alaskan brown bear, largest North American carnivore, and the black bear inhabit the monument. Thousands of Canada geese nest on the Gustavus Point area of the reservation.

The regional director of Region Four, National Park Service, San Francisco 5, California, is in charge of the monument. Accommodations have not yet been provided.

GRAND CANYON NATIONAL MONUMENT, in northern Arizona, is adjacent

to Grand Canyon National Primeval Park on the west, and comprises an area of 305 square miles. The canyon in the monument is considerably narrower than that in the park, and outstanding features are the lava flows that poured over the canyon's rim damming the river during a period of volcanic activity. Wildlife, plant life, coloring and general appearance are similar to those of the park. The monument is administered by the superintendent of Grand Canyon National Primeval Park. It is not yet accessible to the general public.

GREAT SAND DUNES NATIONAL MONUMENT, in south central Colorado,

consisting of fifty-seven square miles of sand dunes, was established in 1932. Carried by the prevailing westerly winds, the sand has been heaped up along the west base of the Sangre de Cristo Mountains to form the largest dunes in the United States. Nearly a thousand feet high, these rippled, brownish gray silica dunes offer a striking contrast to the forest-covered, snow-capped mountains that rise 14,000 feet above sea

Glacier Bay National Monument is an area of snow-capped peaks, glaciers and arms of the sea. It is forested at the lowest altitudes and supports an abundant wildlife population. Of special interest to scientists is the opportunity to study post-glacial establishment of flora, for the glaciers are receding a little each year.

National Park Service

The Great Sand Dunes, heaped along the base of Colorado's Sangre de Cristo Mountains, raise their shifting crests almost a thousand feet above the valley floor.

level. Mount Cleveland, the highest peak in the range, stands directly behind the dunes. To the west across the San Luis Valley in which the dunes are located, are the La Garita and San Juan ranges. Geologists say that the Sangre de Cristo Mountains comprise a fault-block, earth-forces having broken and lifted them upward from the level of the valley floor. At one time the valley was filled with a lake, but this later drained off through a channel on the south, and today the valley is semi-arid. Flowing from the snows of the high peaks is the Medano River. This stream skirts the dunes for several miles, finally disappearing into the sand. Near the southwestern edge of the dunes are a pond and springs believed to be the re-emergence of the water of the Medano. During migration, large numbers of ducks visit these waters. The only plant life in the dunes is a species of sunflower that grows in moist depressions.

The monument is under the care of the regional director, Region Three, National Park Service, Santa Fe, New Mexico. There are no visitor accommodations in the monument, but these are available at nearby towns. The reservation is reached from U. S. Highway 160 at Alamosa, Colorado, then north over State Route 17 to Mosca, and from there over State Route 150 east to the monument. The monument is open all year.

JACKSON HOLE NATIONAL MONUMENT adjoins the eastern and northern boundaries of Grand Teton National Primeval Park and is six miles south of Yellowstone National Primeval Park in northwestern Wyoming. It was established in 1943, and comprises an area of 346 square miles of sage flats, forests, grasslands and lakes. Although essentially level, the area contains buttes and glacial moraines. The largest lake in the monument, Jackson Lake, on the Snake River, is dammed at its outlet and the water used for irrigation down stream. The Snake River winds through the monument from north to south, and is joined by the Buffalo Fork in the north, and by

The diversity of ridges, terraces, channels, and depressions gives Jackson Hole its distinctive quality of landscape; and geologically these features are significant as records of the Glacial Period when Jackson Hole was the meeting ground for glaciers.

the Gros Ventre River which flows across the south end of the monument. Jackson Hole is hemmed in by two ranges of mountains. On the east are the Gros Ventre Mountains, partly forested, and having gentle, rounded outlines. On the west rises abruptly the jagged, pale gray Teton Range, in Grand Teton National Primeval Park, forested on its lower slopes and rising far above timber line to a height of 13,766 feet above sea level and standing more than 7000 feet above the floor of Jackson Hole.

This view shows the northeastern part of Jackson Hole National Monument with Signal Mountain at left and Jackson Lake and the Teton peaks in the distance.

Jackson Hole with its winding rivers, sage flats and woodlands, is a wild and unspoiled setting from which to view the Teton peaks in Grand Teton National Primeval Park. Massive Mount Moran is shown here reflected in the Snake River.

Geologically this valley is called a fault-trough, while the Tetons are known as a fault-block range. In early geologic times, a fracture developed in the earth approximately along the western edge of the valley. The land on the west side was lifted to form the Tetons, while that on the east was lowered. Geologists are able to study here the activities of ancient glaciers believed to have descended into the valley at three different times, over a period as long as two million years. Among the mammals are the moose, elk, coyote, black bear and beaver, while included among the birds are Wilson snipe, Lincoln sparrow, hermit thrush, Barrow's golden-eye duck, trumpeter swan and sage grouse. Important tree species are the whitebark, limber and lodgepole pine, Engelmann and Colorado blue spruce, alpine and Douglas fir, cottonwood and quaking aspen. Some of the several hundred flowering plants are the balsam root, scarlet gilia, larkspur, wild buckwheat, Indian paintbush, lupine, pentstemon, purple fringe, bitterbrush, service berry, honeysuckle and mountain balm.

Cattle grazing is now permitted in the monument, but when this is eliminated the vegetation along cattle driveways will be restored. An area, in part privately owned, of 1200 acres near Moran within the monument is being developed by scientific societies as a research laboratory for the study of elk, deer, antelope and other mammals. While it is the expressed policy of the National Park Service that "presentation of the animal life of the parks to the public shall be a wholly natural one," the animals in this project, although restricted under artificial conditions, will be serving the useful purpose of providing scientific information on wildlife problems.

The monument is administered jointly with Grand Teton National Primeval Park, and the headquarters address is Moose, Wyoming. Accommodations are available at numerous ranches throughout the monument and at a hotel in nearby Jackson. The monument is reached over U. S. Highway 89 south from Yellowstone National Primeval Park and north from Ogden and Logan, Utah; also over U. S. Highway 287 from Rawlins, Wyoming. East from Victor, Idaho, State Route 22 runs to Jackson via scenic Teton Pass. Yellowstone Park Company busses provide service between Yellowstone, Grand Teton and the monument. There is also bus service from Victor to Moran in the monument. The Union Pacific Railroad leaves visitors at Victor and at West Yellowstone, Montana, and the Northern Pacific at the Gardner entrance of Yellowstone Park; while the Chicago, Burlington and Quincy leaves visitors at Cody, Wyoming, whence there is bus service to Yellowstone Park. The monument is open from June 15 to September 15.

JEWEL CAVE NATIONAL MONUMENT, in southwestern South Dakota, was established in 1908. It consists of a little over two square miles, having as its chief feature a limestone cavern with walls encrusted with glittering spar calcite crystals. The cavern is made up of many rooms connected by passages with side galleries. One of the passageways is inhabited by a colony of lumpnosed bats. The area above ground contains one of the finest remaining stands of ponderosa pine in the Black Hills.

The monument is under the care of the superintendent of Wind Cave National Park. The address is Hot Springs, South Dakota. It is reached on U. S. Highway 16 fourteen miles west of Custer, South Dakota, and twenty-three miles east of Newcastle, Wyoming. The Chicago, Burlington and Quincy Railroad serves Custer. There is a campground in the monument, while other accommodations are available at Custer. The cave is open daily from June 1 to September 30.

JOSHUA TREE NATIONAL MONUMENT, in southern California, was established in 1936 to preserve part of the Mojave and Colorado deserts. Comprising an area of 1344 square miles, one of its chief features is a stand of the large yucca known as the Joshua tree. Throughout its limited range in this part of California, western Arizona, Nevada and southern Utah, the Joshua tree is diminishing because of cattle grazing and because commercial uses are being made of its fibers. The stand within the monument is unspoiled and deserves the protection now afforded it. This tree, one of the

The chief feature of Joshua Tree National Monument is the stand of Joshua trees in Lost Horse Valley. Beavertail cactus, with its crimson flowers, is one of the species needing the protection of the monument. Outside of the desert monuments, cacti and other succulents are being taken for ornamental purposes and by florists and hobbyists and for sale in five and ten-cent stores. Thus, with the deserts being depleted of one of their attractive features, the necessity of maintaining these national monuments takes on added importance.

George A. Grant

Joshua Tree National Monument, in California's Mojave Desert, established to protect a stand of the weird Joshua tree, is today in danger of despoilment by mining interests and by the existence of private lands within the reservation.

weirdest species of North America's flora, attains heights up to forty feet. Its foliage consists of dense clusters of stiff, dull green, sharp-pointed leaves, and its blossoms, large heads of creamy white flowers appearing in spring, are borne at the branch terminals. The monument's mammals are the desert bighorn, mule deer, coyote, badger, bobcat, kit and gray fox and jack rabbit.

Parts of the monument, as originally established, contain no Joshua trees and here mining and other commercial activities have disturbed the primeval desert. A bill to exclude these tracts from the monument was introduced but not passed in the 79th Congress. Such exclusion would be desirable, since disturbed areas do not belong within a national monument of this character. Joshua Tree National Monument has been faced with two serious dangers. The heart of the monument, the Joshua tree forest, is still checkerboarded with privately owned lands. Since Congress failed to appropriate funds for their purchase by the federal government, the owners may sell to buyers whose interests will run counter to the nature preservation concept. This could result in the despoilment and loss of the monument. A second danger lies in the fact that mining interests covet the entire area. If this esthetically and scientifically important monument is to be preserved intact, it may require the combined force of thinking Americans demanding that Congress appropriate funds for federal acquisition of the private in-holdings.

Headquarters is at Twentynine Palms, California. Accommodations are available at Twentynine Palms, Joshua Tree, Yucca Valley, Palm Springs and Indio. There are none at the monument. The area is reached over U. S. Highway 66 east from Barstow and west from Needles, California, to Amboy, where a side road runs southwest forty miles to Twentynine Palms. It is reached also over U. S. highways 60, 70 and 99 east from Los Angeles and Riverside to White Water where a road leads to the monument entrances at Twentynine Palms and Joshua Tree; and west from Phoenix, Arizona, and Blythe, California, over the same route to Indio. Summer visitors should inquire of local travel agencies as to road conditions, because flash floods from thunderstorms frequently wash out sections of the road. The Southern Pacific Railroad serves Indio. The monument is open all year.

KATMAI NATIONAL MONUMENT, located on the southeast coast of the Alaska Peninsula, was established in 1918. It consists of 4214 square miles, and is the largest area administered by the National Park Service. Chief features are the crater of Katmai Volcano and the Valley of Ten Thousand Smokes. The region was explored by expeditions sent out by the National Geographic Society shortly after the eruption of Katmai in 1912, one of the half dozen most violent during recorded history. A brief eye-witness account by a native of Savanoski village, twenty miles north of the volcano, describes the flight of the villagers by boat to Naknek in the darkness caused by the clouds of hot, falling ash. Kodiak, a hundred miles away, was buried under a foot of ashes. The concussion of the eruption was audible 750 miles away and, throughout the northern hemisphere, the sun was dimmed for months by the dust. The crater of Katmai is eight miles in circumference and contains a mile-wide lake of milky blue water with a crescent-shaped island of forty acres. Five miles northwest of the volcano lies the Valley of Ten Thousand Smokes. When discovered in 1916, this area, about the size of the District of Columbia, contained millions of steam jets, some rising more than a thousand feet. The valley was filled by a flow of incandescent pumice, sand and ash.

Today the volcanic activity of this unearthly valley has largely died down, although the volcano, Mt. Mageik, located within the monument, is active. The monument lies at the Arctic edge of the coniferous forest where white spruce predominates. Other tree species are balsam poplar, paper birch, quaking aspen and cottonwood. The mountain and lake scenery is unsurpassed. Most noteworthy of the mammals of the monument

Katmai Volcano erupted in 1912, and was one of the dozen greatest eruptions known. Towns a hundred miles away were covered with a foot of ash, and the concussion was felt 750 miles distant. As is plainly visible, only a stump of the mountain remains, the top having been blown off leaving a huge crater.

Robert F. Griggs

Mount Mageik, one of the big mountains of Katmai Monument, is still active. Although these slopes are barren, much of the monument is covered with forest and the area constitutes an outstanding wildlife reservation, the largest administered by the National Park Service.

is the Alaska brown bear, the largest North American carnivore. Also inhabiting the monument are the moose, caribou, red, cross and silver fox, wolverine, wolf, marten, mink, otter, beaver and lynx. Ducks, geese, swans, loons and grebes inhabit the lakes and streams, while the forests and grasslands provide habitat for Steller jay, northern shrike, red crossbill, arctic three-toed woodpecker, robin, golden-crowned sparrow, varied thrush and grouse. Salmon occur in great numbers, breeding in the lakes. Over many square miles beyond the forest border, the ground is covered by a rich growth of native red top grass which stands seven feet high.

The monument is administered through the superintendent of Mount McKinley National Primeval Park, Alaska, and has not yet been made accessible to visitors.

LAVA BEDS NATIONAL MONUMENT, in northern California, was established in 1925 to preserve an area of seventy-one square miles of volcanic formations. The most recent activity is believed to have taken place 5000 years ago. Within the area are numerous caves, or lava tubes, formed when the surface of lava flows cooled and solidified, while the inner liquid continued to flow and seep away, leaving the hollow tube. The roofs and sides of these tubes vary greatly. Some are the color of chocolate, and are covered with drippings that form strange patterns. In places the walls are lined with shelves and ripples. Skull Cave contains a small room that is floored with ice. The entrance to this cave is big enough to hold a large house, while the roof of Catacomb Cave is so low that one can reach up and touch it in many places. Fern Cave, the walls of which are adorned with ancient Indian paintings, has a garden of ferns and mosses on its floor, although these plant forms occur nowhere else in this semi-arid region. Other caves with descriptive names are Indian Well Cave, Silver Cave, Dragon's Head and White Lace Cave. About 130 caves have been explored. The monument varies from 4000 to 5000 feet above sea level and comprises a remarkably rugged and broken terrain. In the monument there are also cinder cones, spatter cones or chimneys, two lava fields— the Black Lava Flow and Devil's Homestead; and there are several natural bridges.

Besides these fascinating geologic features, the area contains a varied mammal

The Devil's Homestead is one of the two large black lava flows in Lava Beds National Monument. This flow is well known to visitors because the road through the monument runs across it.

Devereux Butcher

Devereux Butcher

Skull Cave is one of the largest lava caves in Lava Beds
National Monument. It was so named because skulls of
the now extinct Lava Beds bighorn sheep were found in
the cave where Indians used to corner the animals and kill
them for food. Far down in the depths of the cave there is
a small room with a floor of ice. The monument's
custodian standing on the trail at right lends scale.

and bird population, while the plant life is equally varied. Thousands of Rocky Mountain mule deer winter on the reservation. Other mammals are the coyote, bobcat, badger, porcupine, jack rabbit, ground squirrel and chipmunk. The Lava Beds bighorn sheep once lived here, but is now extinct. Among the birds there are the California and mountain quail, mourning dove, green-tailed towhee, Audubon's warbler, Pacific night-hawk, California jay, several species of hummingbirds, flycatchers, linnets, hawks and owls. Trees are chiefly the fragrant western cedar and the ponderosa pine. Shrubs include such species as bitter bush, sage, mountain mahogany, and the fern bush which has lacy, fragrant leaves and white flowers. Smaller plants are the California poppy, Indian paintbrush, wild flax, pentstemon, sulphur flower and the pale lavender mariposa lily. In a small disconnected part of the monument known as Petroglyph Cliff, there are hundreds of prehistoric petroglyphs or pictorial carvings. In 1872-73, the Modoc War, one of the last stands of the Modoc Indians against the white men, took place in the lava beds. The Indians, making use of caves and fissures providing almost impregnable fortifications, were able to inflict severe losses upon the white man's forces.

Headquarters is within the monument, and the address is Tulelake, California. There are campgrounds in the reservation. Other accommodations are available at Klamath Falls and Merrill, Oregon, and Tulelake. The monument is reached south from Klamath Falls over State Route 39, and north from Canby, California, on U. S. Highway 299 where State Route 39 branches north to the monument. Lava Beds is situated about midway between Crater Lake and Lassen Volcanic national primeval parks. When overnight accommodations have been established at the monument, and the roads within the monument have been improved, the area will provide a logical stopover and a point of high interest for tourists traveling between these two parks. The monument is open all year.

LEHMAN CAVES NATIONAL MONUMENT, in eastern Nevada, was established in 1922. Comprising an area of one square mile, its chief feature is a limestone cave discovered by Abe Lehman in the early 1870's. The cavern, surrounded by the Nevada National Forest, is located on the eastern slope of Wheeler Peak, 13,058 feet, highest in the Snake Range. The cave is about 7000 feet above sea level in the belt of pinyon pine and juniper where, even though surrounded by one of the most arid regions of the United States, mountain streams flow all year. The geologic setting of the cavern is a metamorphic limestone probably belonging to the middle Cambrian Period. Hundreds of thousands of years ago water charged with carbon-dioxide seeped through cracks dissolving the limestone until the cracks widened into rooms and passages. In the cave are stalagmites and stalactites, drapery and ribbon-like formations and disks called tom-toms because, when struck, they resound like a drum. On the floors of the cavern are terraced pools with delicately formed dikes, while on the walls, ceilings and on some of the larger formations, there are incrustations of needle crystals and mushroom-like nodules of infinite variety. Coloring ranges from chocolate through buff to cream white. The trip through the cave over easy-graded trails, is a half mile. On the monument's above-ground area there are deer, mountain lion, coyote, owls and jays.

The monument is under the care of the superintendent of the Boulder Dam Recreation Area, Boulder City, Nevada, who is represented by a resident custodian with headquarters at Baker, Nevada. On the reservation a campground near headquarters has been provided for those who bring their own equipment. Hotels and other accommodations are available at Ely, Nevada. The monument is reached over U. S. Highway 6 about fifty miles east of Ely to a road that branches south near Sacramento Pass sixteen miles to the monument. From Hinkley, Utah, it is reached about one hundred miles west on the same route. The monument is open all year.

MUIR WOODS NATIONAL MONUMENT, comprising an area of two-thirds of a square mile, was established in 1908. The tract was given to the nation by the late

The main trail in Muir Woods winds among towering coast redwood trees and tall clumps of azaleas
growing on the floor of a steep-walled canyon.

Congressman William Kent and his wife, Elizabeth Thatcher Kent, and was named for the naturalist, John Muir. Prior to establishment as a national monument, it was planned to log the area and use its canyon as a reservoir. Located near the California coast ten miles north of the Golden Gate Bridge, its chief feature is a grove of coast redwood trees, *Sequoia sempervirens*. This species is related to the sequoia, *Sequoia gigantea*, of Yosemite, Kings Canyon and Sequoia national primeval parks, but it differs from the latter in several respects. The foliage of the redwood somewhat resembles that of hemlock, while the sequoia foliage is more like that of cedar. The redwood grows taller than the sequoia, many trees exceeding 300 feet, but it does not develop as large a trunk diameter. *Sempervirens* grows from sprouts or seeds, and it is not uncommon to see young trees growing in a circle that marks the base of an ancient monarch long since rotted away. In the monument the tall straight trunks of the redwoods are in striking contrast to the leaning, mossy trunks of bay, false nutmeg, tanbark oak, bigleaf maple and madrone with its bright colored bark and broad evergreen leaves. Other important trees of the reservation are Douglas fir and California buckeye, the latter forming a dense, rounded crown on which large, conspicuous spikes of white blossoms appear in summer. There are such plants as violet, shooting star, deer-tongue, oxalis, salal, clintonia, trillium, as well as azalea, sweet vernal or vanilla grass, and ferns.

Black-tailed deer, gray fox, wildcat, raccoon and Douglas squirrel inhabit the forest. The varied thrush, Steller jay, Allen and Anna hummingbirds, California quail, winter wren, Marin chickadee and other avian species are found here. Along the floor of the canyon winds a stream and a broad trail with picnic areas at intervals. Other trails climb the forested canyon walls to the grassy wind-swept ridges above. Muir Woods is a superbly beautiful sylvan spot. On the monument's west, north and east borders it adjoins the much larger Mount Tamalpais State Park.

Headquarters is within the monument, and the address is Mill Valley, California. Lunches are available within the monument. There are no overnight or camping accommodations, and visitors leave before dark. No fires are permitted. The monument is reached from the north over U. S. Highway 101 to Mill Valley where a road branches southwest five miles to the monument. Coming north from San Francisco on U. S. Highway 101, a side road to the monument forks to the right three miles north of Golden Gate Bridge. Greyline busses take visitors from San Francisco to the monument. The reservation is open all year.

NATURAL BRIDGES NATIONAL MONUMENT, in colorful southeastern Utah,

was established in 1908. The monument, including four square miles in three disconnected areas, contains three sandstone bridges that are the result of stream erosion. The largest, Sipapu Bridge, is 222 feet above the stream bed, has a span of 261 feet, and is 128 feet wide and sixty-five feet thick at its smallest point. Kachina Bridge, the most massive of the three, has a span of 186 feet, is forty-nine feet wide and 107 feet thick at the smallest point, and stands 205 feet above the stream. Owachomo Bridge, the smallest, is 108 feet high with a span of 194 feet, thirty-five feet wide and ten feet thick at its center. Geologists say that these bridges were carved during centuries by running water, the bridges formerly having been solid walls located at sharp bends in the rivers where the constant grinding of sand-laden water swirled against them and wore them through. Besides these three marvelous examples of erosion, there are within the monument two large caves and a number of cliff dwellings. The latter, high in the walls of the canyon, are difficult to reach. The terminus of the road to the monument is at Owachomo Bridge. The other two bridges must be reached on foot or horseback, which involves a round trip of nine miles through spectacular country.

The monument is under the care of the regional director, Region Three, National Park Service, Santa Fe, New Mexico, who is represented by a resident ranger in summer. The address is Blanding, Utah. The monument is reached over U. S. Highway 160 from north and east to Monticello, Utah, where State Route 47 runs south to Blanding, there

Sipapu Bridge, 222 feet above the stream bed of White Canyon, is the largest and most beautifully proportioned of the bridges in Natural Bridges National Monument, Utah.

joining the highly scenic State Route 95 that runs fifty miles to the monument. The monument is open in summer, and in winter when road conditions permit.

OREGON CAVES NATIONAL MONUMENT, established in 1909, is located at 4000 feet above sea level in the Siskiyou Mountains of southwestern Oregon, and is surrounded by the Siskiyou National Forest. Chief feature of the area are caves of winding passages and rooms with calcite formations. Believed to have been discovered by Elijah Davidson in 1874, the caves originated far back in geologic history. The region once was the bed of an ocean upon which was laid a deposit of lime. Hardening into limestone, this was later uplifted to form a range of mountains. Under great pressure and heat during this period, the limestone was changed to marble that was cracked in being raised. Water charged with carbonic acid seeped through the cracks, and then began the slow action of dissolving the marble. Gradually the cracks widened until the caverns were formed and the water, depositing the lime in solution wherever it dripped, built up the stalactites, stalagmites and other formations. The walk through the caverns extends a mile and a quarter. Although Oregon Caves lack the spectacular beauty and color of many other caves, the room known as Paradise Lost is outstanding. The floor space in this room is narrow, but the ceiling rises to a great height, and the walls are hung with fantastic head-like formations. The reservation includes two-thirds of a square mile. The forest of the area, with many fine trails, is composed of sugar pine, Douglas fir, western hemlock, weeping spruce, madrone, tanbark oak, and rhododendron that bears bright pink flowers. Black bear and mule deer are sometimes seen.

The monument is administered by the superintendent of Crater Lake National Primeval Park, who is represented by a resident ranger in summer. The Oregon Caves Chateau, situated at the entrance to the caves, provides accommodations for visitors.

Head-like formations of calcite cover the walls of the room called
Paradise Lost in Oregon's marble caverns. Located high in the
Siskiyou Mountains, this reservation lies within the range of the rare
weeping spruce, a tall conifer having long, pendulous twigs. The
spruce is native to these mountains, and nowhere else in the world.
Here, too, grows the madrone, a broadleaved evergreen with smooth
reddish bark, and the tanbark oak which makes a striking show
when in bloom during late July. The unusual beauty of the forest
along the last eight miles to the caves alone repays one for the visit.

There are no campgrounds on the reservation, but these are available nearby in the national forest. The monument is reached over U. S. Highway 199 north from Crescent City, California, and south from Grants Pass, Oregon, to Cave Junction, Oregon, where State Route 46 branches east twenty miles to the monument. The Oregon Caves Resort Company provides bus service between Cave Junction and the caves, making connection with the buses of the Pacific Greyhound Company during the summer travel season, and on call during the off season. The reservation is convenient for tourists traveling between Crater Lake National Primeval Park and California's redwood state parks. The monument is open all year, but regular guide service through the caves is provided only from May 29 to October 1. In winter, guides are available at higher rates whenever visitors desire to go through the caves.

ORGAN PIPE CACTUS NATIONAL MONUMENT, situated on the international border in southwestern Arizona, was established in 1937. The area comprises 516 square miles of Sonoran Desert with an unsurpassed desert flora as its chief feature. In addition, it has a faunal population of high esthetic and scientific interest. The country within the monument is dominated by five mountain ranges rising abruptly from the desert floor to splintered peaks with elevations of 5000 feet. The organ pipe cactus, for which the area is named, is one of the more abundant species found there. However, it grows only on south slopes, while the larger saguaro cactus is more abundant. The organ pipe has numerous ribbed and spined columnar branches that rise at or close to the ground and attain heights of from five to twenty-five feet. The flowers, which bloom at night, are borne near the upper ends of the columns, and generally range from brownish through green to white. Other cactus species are the night-blooming cereus, or *reina de la noche*, one or two and rarely eight feet tall, with large white flowers that are strongly perfumed, opening after sundown about the end of June or in July; the hedgehog cactus,

Teddy bear cactus (left) has blooms of green, yellow or white streaked with lavender, while the flowers of organ pipe cactus, opening at night, are brownish, green or white. Both species inhabit Organ Pipe Cactus National Monument, Arizona.

George A. Grant

Organ Pipe Cactus National Monument is not only
a veritable botanic garden of Sonoran desert life,
but is scenically interesting. This view, taken
from the Sonoita Hills, shows the Ajo Mountains.

forming clusters of cylindrical stems six to twenty-four inches high, thickly spined and
bearing flowers with crimson petals and yellow centers; the Wislizenius barrel cactus,
a comparatively large species that consists usually of a single ribbed stem from two to
four and sometimes six feet high and from one to two feet in diameter, thickly spined
along the ribs, and bearing orange-red or yellow flowers set in a ring on the apex of
the plant. Cactus fruit, particularly of the latter species, provides food for several forms
of wildlife. Crucifixion thorn, palo verde, creosote bush, ocotillo, ironwood, mesquite,
bur-sage, catclaw, smoke tree and desert willow also grow in the monument.

Among the mammals, there are desert bighorn sheep, gray and kit fox, jack
rabbit, coyote, pronghorn antelope, Arizona whitetail deer, desert mule deer, burro
deer and Mexican red deer, badger, peccary and coati-mundi. Among the birds are the
white-winged, Inca and western mourning dove, Gambel's quail, canyon and cactus wren,
phainopepla, Arizona cardinal, vermilion flycatcher, raven and roadrunner. Eagles and
hawks are frequently seen.

Cattle grazing, which has no rightful place in any nature reservation, has not yet
been eliminated from this monument, and is causing great damage. Such damage results
in the breakdown of the larger shrubs and trees, and in the trampling of smaller
vegetation, contributing to soil erosion.

Headquarters is at Ajo, Arizona, on State Route 85 eighteen miles from the monument entrance. There are no accommodations for visitors in the monument, but there
are hotels, restaurants and cabins at Ajo and Gila Bend, Arizona. The monument is
reached from Tucson, Arizona, over State Route 84 to Gila Bend, then south through
Ajo on State Route 85, paved the entire distance; or over the more interesting, but only
partly paved road west through the Papago Indian Reservation. From Phoenix and
Yuma, Arizona, it is reached over U. S. Highway 80 to Gila Bend. The Southern Pacific
and Santa Fe railroads serve Phoenix, and the Southern Pacific serves Tucson. The
monument is open all year.

PETRIFIED FOREST NATIONAL MONUMENT, in eastern Arizona, was established in 1906. Comprising an area of 145 square miles, its chief feature is the largest and most colorful collection of petrified wood in the world. This once was a living forest. Scientists believe that the trees of the forest belonged to the upper Triassic Period 160 million to 170 million years ago, when northern Arizona was near the sea. The trees died of natural causes and were transported by a stream into the flood plain. Here they settled in the sand and became waterlogged, eventually being buried beneath deposits of sand and shale which excluded oxygen, thus preventing rotting. In this way, there was time to permit petrifaction—the formation of carnelian, agate, jasper, onyx and opal.

The petrified forest was discovered in 1851, but the area remained almost unknown until 1878. The Santa Fe Railroad, which runs through the reservation, was completed in 1883, and it was after that date that jewelers, gem collectors, souvenir hunters and manufacturers of abrasives began to carry off the petrified wood which served their needs because of its hardness, bright colors and ability to take a high polish. With one of the rarest exhibits of nature's handiwork in imminent danger of annihilation, the people of Arizona petitioned Congress to make a reservation of the area and place it under federal protection. Within the monument the remnants of trees lie scattered on the ground. There are the First, Second, Third, Rainbow, Blue and Black forests, varying in color, and these, together with a large part of the Painted Desert added to the monument in 1932, constitute a reservation of great scientific and esthetic importance. Agate House, an ancient Indian ruin in the monument, is also an attraction for visitors.

Although desert conditions prevail, several species of mammals inhabit the area. These include the pronghorn antelope, bobcat, badger, cottontail and jack rabbit, coyote, porcupine, prairie dog, spotted and Arizona skunk, fox, pack rat and antelope ground squirrel. Among the plants are golden sego lily, mariposa lily, yucca, globemallow,

Petrified Forest National Monument contains a small part of the famous Painted Desert. The hills in this view are predominantly white or yellowish, pink and deep red.

Devereux Butcher

In the foreground are the broken segments of a petrified tree trunk long ago eroded from the desert's clay. Farther back, another trunk, still unbroken, is nearly unearthed. On the hillside a third is just beginning to appear.

The volcanic spires of Pinnacles National
Monument rise above a rugged and picturesque country that is the habitat of many
species of wildlife, both mammals and birds.

Colorado four o'clock, evening primrose, several species of sage and five species of cactus. There are numerous shrubs, including black greasewood, skunkbush, rabbit bush and oneseed juniper.

Headquarters is in the monument, and the address is Holbrook, Arizona. There are two museums in the monument. Accommodations for visitors are provided at the Rainbow Forest Lodge and at Painted Desert Inn at the north entrance. There is also a campground for those who bring their own equipment and there are cabins near the south entrance. The monument is reached over U. S. Highway 66 east from Flagstaff, Arizona, and west from Gallup, New Mexico, the route passing through the monument. U. S. Highway 260, which joins U. S. Highway 66 at Holbrook, passes the south entrance nineteen miles southeast of Holbrook. The Santa Fe Railroad leaves visitors at Holbrook where cars are available for trips through the monument. The monument is open all year.

PINNACLES NATIONAL MONUMENT, in west central California, an area of twenty square miles of eroded domes, spires and caves of volcanic origin, was established in 1908. Formations rise to heights of from 500 to 1200 feet above the intervening canyons. A good trail system traverses the canyons, scenic cliffs and pinnacles, and winds up Chalone Peak, highest point in the reservation, 3287 feet above sea level. Digger pines grow along the dry, chaparral-covered slopes, and there are live oaks in the deep canyons and ravines. Wildlife includes deer, raccoon, gray fox, coyote, bobcat, ground squirrel, cottontail rabbit and pack rat, the latter occasionally making its presence known as it vibrates its tail against some object. Among the birds there are the duck hawk, prairie falcon, golden eagle, turkey vulture, California quail, white-throated swift, violet-green, tree and cliff swallow, California woodpecker, rock wren, western bluebird and white-crowned and golden-crowned sparrow.

Headquarters is in the monument, and the address is Pinnacles, California. The monument is reached over State Route 25 thirty-five miles from Hollister, California, on the north, and the same distance from King City, California, on the south. It is also reached over U. S. Highway 101 south from Salinas to Soledad and east on a branch road four miles to the monument. Cabins and meals are available at Pinnacles Lodge in the monument. The reservation is open all year.

RAINBOW BRIDGE NATIONAL MONUMENT is located in arid, scenic southeastern Utah within the Paiute Indian Reservation just north of the Arizona line. The area, consisting of a quarter square mile, was established in 1910 to protect the colossal arch rising 309 feet above the floor of Bridge Canyon. The arch, almost twice as high as Niagara Falls, is called *Barahoini* by the Paiute Indians, a word meaning "the rainbow" derived from its rainbow-like symmetry. The setting of Rainbow Bridge is spectacular. On either side, canyon walls of red sandstone tower to heights two or three times as great as that of the bridge itself. When seen from afar in the huge canyon, the bridge appears insignificant in size. The bridge was once a solid narrow wall at a bend in Bridge Creek. Through centuries of wearing by sand-laden water, the creek broke through the wall and took a short cut. For centuries more erosion widened the opening until only the top of the wall remains today in the form of the arch.

The monument is under the care of the regional director, Region Three, National Park Service, Santa Fe, New Mexico. Accommodations for visitors are available at Rainbow Lodge, Arizona. From here the ten-mile horseback trip to the monument is made. Rainbow Lodge is reached over a road that branches east from U. S. Highway 89 at a point ten miles north of Cameron, Arizona, going through Tuba City and Tonalea, Arizona, and turning north six miles from the latter town to the lodge. The Santa Fe Railroad serves Grand Canyon National Primeval Park, and the Fred Harvey Company provides automobile service from Grand Canyon to Rainbow Lodge, a five-day round trip. The monument is open all year.

One of the great spectacles of nature is the red sandstone
Rainbow Bridge, an arch of almost rainbow symmetry, carved
for centuries by water, and standing 309 feet above the canyon
floor. Two visitors quench a desert thirst at the pool's edge.

The coyote is an intelligent and often handsome animal. Whether he is heard vocalizing at night or seen in his daytime wanderings, he is an attractive rascal deserving the protection given him in the parks and monuments. Although killed by livestock interests outside the nature reservations, he seems able to maintain himself. There is need for wider understanding of the valuable service performed by predators under natural conditions. As the complex principles of predation become better known, the coyote and other predators will be appreciated as worthy, interesting members of the native North American faunal population.

W. M. Sharp for
Fish and Wildlife Service

The gray fox is at home in the scrub and chaparral of the southwestern desert national monuments, including Saguaro, and in the forests below 5,000 feet northward to Crater Lake and Dinosaur National Monument. The red fox, more wary than the gray, inhabits the Sierra and Rocky Mountain parks north to Mount McKinley in Alaska and east to the Appalachian national parks. The kit fox is a native of the desert national monuments. Smaller than the other two, the kit fox is much less shy, and consequently, outside the monuments, his numbers have been greatly reduced and he deserves protection.

A. M. Pearson for
Fish and Wildlife Service

The saguaro cactus, having large waxy white or cream colored blossoms with cupped centers of bright yellow anthers, forms stands as dense as forest trees.

SAGUARO NATIONAL MONUMENT, in southern Arizona, was established in 1933. Ninety-eight square miles in extent, its chief feature is a superb forest of the giant saguaro cactus, which has its range in southwestern Arizona and Sonora, Mexico. The plant, with its ribbed columns and thousands of spines, is slow in growth, and may reach a height of only three feet in thirty years, yet many specimens have attained heights up to fifty feet. The blossom of the saguaro, opening at night during May, has large waxy white to cream colored petals and a cupped center of bright yellow anthers. The flowers are borne in a mass covering the ends of the upward-reaching branches. Other species of cactus are prickly pear, consisting of spined pads that bear yellow flowers and edible fruits called "tunas"; hedgehog, consisting of small cucumber-like plants that produce crimson blossoms with yellow centers; barrel, resembling young unbranched saguaro six feet in height with yellow or orange flowers; and several species of cholla, sometimes called tree cactus, bearing yellow, red or orange flowers. Other plants of the area are palo verde, a small tree that has green bark, very small leaves and is covered with bright yellow flowers in spring; creosote bush; mesquite; ocotillo, a plant consisting of thorny whips eight to fifteen feet long that branch at the ground and which are tipped with scarlet flowers in spring.

Wildlife of the reservation is interestingly varied and includes the coyote, desert mule deer, peccary, black bear, ringtail, gray fox, kangaroo rat, raccoon, jack rabbit, Harris ground squirrel and badger. The white-winged dove, Inca dove, Mexican ground dove, western mourning dove, and the elf owl, no larger than a sparrow, inhabit the monument. For nest sites the elf owl uses abandoned holes in the saguaro made by the gilded flicker and Gila woodpecker. Other birds are the cactus wren, the desert screech owl,

National Park Service, courtesy American Planning and Civic Ass'n.

During spring, the desert of Saguaro National Monument is a garden of bright cactus blooms. Above are the large white flowers of the night-bloom-ing cereus. Lower left are the white and yellow blooms of the giant saguaro, while at right one of the pincushion species wears a crown of its blossoms.

National Park Service

several species of thrashers including the Crissal, Bendire's, and Palmer; also the white-rumped shrike, Say's phoebe, Arizona crested flycatcher, Arizona cardinal, Scott's oriole, phainopepla, pyrrhuloxia and western mockingbird. There are several species of snakes including the red and black phases of the western red racers, several species of rattlesnakes and, at higher elevations, the kingsnake. Among the more common lizards are the black and pink Gila monster, the chuckawalla in rocky locations, the collared lizard and the desert scaly lizard.

Today the existence of the saguaro is threatened by the grazing of cattle which, on private and state owned unfenced lands within the monument, has not been eliminated. It is also threatened by a bacterium that attacks and kills the oldest plants. Aggressive public opposition to continued livestock grazing within the monument is necessary. The removal of livestock from the monument will permit restoration of conditions favoring the growth of new plants of saguaro and other desert flora. However, since there has been no reproduction of the saguaro in the area for fifty years, it is believed by some authorities that the saguaro forest within the monument is doomed. Scientific study of the disease is being carried on by the University of Arizona and the U. S. Department of Agriculture in an effort to discover its cause and to bring it under control. The irrigation and cultivation of wide tracts of desert land, greatly increased during wartime, are factors that make imperative the preservation of typical Sonoran Desert areas like the Saguaro National Monument where at least a remnant of the original desert flora and fauna can be preserved for the enjoyment of future generations.

Headquarters is in the monument, and the address is Tucson, Arizona. There are no accommodations for visitors at the monument, but there are good hotels at Tucson. The reservation, open all year, is reached from Tucson via Broadway, a distance of seventeen miles. The Southern Pacific Railroad serves Tucson.

SHOSHONE CAVERN NATIONAL MONUMENT was established in 1909 to place under federal protection a crystal-encrusted limestone cave located high among the scenic cliffs of Cedar Mountain four miles southwest of Cody in northern Wyoming. The known length of the cavern is half a mile. Many crystals, mostly white, are of varied and interesting forms, but there are no large stalagmites or stalactites in the cave. The largest room in the cavern is forty feet wide and eight feet high. The surface area surrounding the cave's mouth is less than one half square mile. Administered jointly with Yellowstone National Primeval Park, the monument is located forty-nine miles from the Sylvan Pass entrance to the park on U. S. Highway 20. Shoshone Cavern is not open to the public.

SUNSET CRATER NATIONAL MONUMENT, in north central Arizona, was established in 1930. Comprising an area of four square miles, its chief feature is the volcanic cinder cone for which the monument is named. Geologists believe that the cone, 400 feet deep, a quarter mile across and a thousand feet high, may have been formed about 900 years ago and that there has been no activity in the region since that time. The crater's name is derived from the color of the cinders around the upper part, which have a reddish tint resembling the colors of a sunset, the lower part of the cone being dull black. At the west base there are four small, brightly colored spatter cones. The lava in the area bears the appearance of having cooled recently. Besides the cones and lava flows, there is an ice cave in which the air is cold the year around. The tree of the area is the ponderosa pine, a few of which grow inside the crater. In this unfavorable habitat, the tree is gnarled and does not reach its usual great size. Small plants with red flowers, the Arizona or red gilia, cover the cinder slopes.

The monument is administered jointly with Wupatki National Monument, and the address is Tuba Star Route, Flagstaff, Arizona. There are no accommodations in the monument, but they are available at nearby Flagstaff. The reservation is reached over U. S. Highway 89 twelve miles north from Flagstaff to a side road that branches east four miles to the monument. The Santa Fe Railroad serves Flagstaff. The monument, open

Joseph Muench, courtesy Nature Magazine

Located in a region of volcanic remains, Sunset Crater, with its
rim of pinkish cinders, may have been formed as recently as 900
years ago. Wheeler National Monument, also the result of volcanic
activity, is an area of spire-like pinnacles and a network of gorges.

W. J. Hutchinson

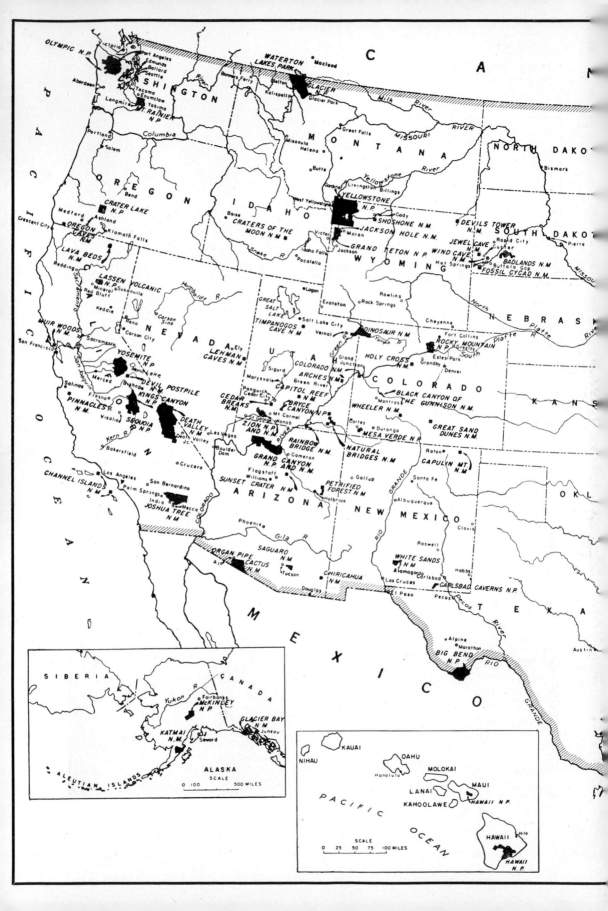

NATIONAL PRIMEVAL PARKS
AND OTHER NATURE RESERVATIONS

ADMINISTERED BY THE NATIONAL PARK SERVICE

SCALE
0   50   100   150   200 MILES

DRAWN FOR NATIONAL PARKS MAGAZINE
By Bess O.M. MacMaugh, 1946

all year except when snow blocks the road in winter, is easily accessible to people driving their own cars to Grand Canyon National Primeval Park. Walnut Canyon and Wupatki national monuments, both containing Indian ruins, are nearby and should be visited on a trip to Sunset Crater.

TIMPANOGOS CAVE NATIONAL MONUMENT, in northern Utah, was established in 1922. It comprises an area of a little more than one-third of a square mile on the northwest slope of Mount Timpanogos in the Wasatch Mountains, and is surrounded by the Wasatch National Forest. Chief feature of the monument consists of three caves, Timpanogos, Middle and Hansen caves, 6776 feet above sea level, which are reached by a mile and a half of steep trails up the American Fork Canyon. Timpanogos Cave, electrically lighted, contains pink and white translucent limestone crystals and small pools of water in which the colorful stalagmites and stalactites are reflected. There are also helictites, formations of vine-like appearance varying from green, blue, lavender, buff and brown to red. This coloring is the result of the presence of iron compounds.

The caves, estimated to be 50 million years old, are faults widened by the dissolving action of water on the limestone. The dripping water, depositing the limestone in solution, created the formations. From the entrance of Timpanogos Cave there are wide views of the Wasatch Mountains and American Fork Canyon. Trees of the monument are white and Douglas fir, cottonwood, boxelder, oak and maple. Bears and deer live in the national forest, and may be seen occasionally by visitors to the monument.

Headquarters is within the reservation, and the address is Pleasant Grove, Utah. There is a picnic area in the monument. Other accommodations are available at American Fork seven miles away. Campgrounds are available in the national forest. The monument is reached over U. S. Highway 91 south from Salt Lake City and north from Provo to American Fork where State Route 80 branches east to the monument. It is reached also over U. S. Highway 40 west from Denver and Steamboat Springs, Colorado, to Heber, Utah, where U. S. Highway 189 branches southwest to a junction with State Route 80 at Wildwood. From Salt Lake City forty miles away, automobiles of the Grayline Bus Company and Utah Motor Tours, leaving at 9 a. m., bring visitors to the monument. The monument is usually open by May 1 and closed November 1.

WHEELER NATIONAL MONUMENT, located in the La Garita Mountains of southern Colorado, comprises a half square mile of volcanic remains and unusual erosion. It was established in 1908 and named in honor of Captain George Wheeler, U. S. Engineers, who in 1874 explored this part of Colorado under direction of the War Department. The area contains fantastic pinnacles and is cut with a maze of gorges. Its eroded mass of gray, brown and black basalt overlying a stratum of volcanic ash presents spectacular scenic beauty enhanced by dense forests of Engelmann spruce mixed with alpine fir. At 11,000 feet above sea level near the crest of the mountains, the reservation is surrounded by the Rio Grande National Forest. Rocky Mountain mule deer, elk and mountain lion are among the mammalian population.

The monument is under the care of the regional director, Region Three, National Park Service, Santa Fe, New Mexico. There is no road into the monument. Wagon Wheel Gap, served by the Denver and Rio Grande Railroad, is nine miles from the monument. The first three miles is by road, and the last six by trail up Bellows Creek. Creede, served by the same railroad, is eight miles away by trail. Guides, saddle and pack horses, camp outfits and supplies are available at Creede. At the monument there is a spring, and a shelter cabin for overnight campers. A fenced pasture is provided for horses. Wagon Wheel Gap and Creede are reached by road east from Durango, Colorado, over U. S. Highway 160 to South Fork, Colorado, where State Route 149 branches northwest seventeen miles. They are reached west from Walsenburg, Colorado, over U. S. Highway 160 to South Fork. The monument is open in summer, but opening and closing dates depend on snow conditions.

White Sands is a name well chosen, for these undulating dunes are as white as snow, being composed of gypsum, the material of which plaster-of-Paris is made.

WHITE SANDS NATIONAL MONUMENT, in southern New Mexico, was established in 1933. It comprises an area of 226 square miles of dunes, some of which are as high as fifty feet. The area is one of unusual beauty because of its pure white, glistening, wind-rippled gypsum sand. Chemically, gypsum is hydrous sulphate of calcium or, as the chemists express it, $CaSO_4\ 2H_2O$. The grains of this sand are large and somewhat resemble granulated sugar or dry snow. Geologists explain that the origin of the dunes is gypsum washed down by seepage from surrounding mountains into the lowest point in the Tularosa Basin which is Lake Lucero on the edge of the dunes. When the water evaporates, the gypsum crystallizes as selenite. The selenite is then reduced to small particles by weathering, swept by the prevailing southwest wind and added to the dunes. Gypsum, also occurring beneath the floor of the Tularosa Basin, is brought to the surface by ground water through capillarity. When the moisture evaporates, gypsum particles remain and become part of the dune sands. These processes are continuing today.

Since the monument extends beyond the sand, mammals such as badger, gray and kit fox, coyote and jack rabbit are present. Some species of insects, lizards and mice found within the white sand area have developed pale or nearly white coloration, making them inconspicuous and protecting them from enemies. Plants able to adapt themselves to the gypsum are rabbit bush, Mormon tea, sand verbena, evening primrose, cottonwood and the creamy flowered yucca. As the dunes encroach, these plants grow long stems to keep their leaves above the sand. A museum occupying a wing of the administration building near the monument entrance, explains fully the origin of the dunes.

Headquarters is within the monument, and the address is Alamogordo, New Mexico. There are no accommodations at the monument, but they are available at Alamogordo, fifteen miles away on U. S. Highway 70, and at Las Cruces, fifty-four miles away on the same route. The Southern Pacific Railroad and Greyhound Bus Lines serve Alamogordo where the White Sands Service Company provides trips to the monument. The monument is open all year.

ZION NATIONAL MONUMENT, an area of seventy-six square miles in southwestern Utah, adjoins Zion National Park on the northwest. It was established in 1937 to protect eight canyons, of which Kolob is the largest and almost as spectacular as Zion Canyon itself. Wildlife, vegetation, geologic origin and coloring are in general similar to those of the national park. The reservation is close to U. S. Highway 91 about twenty miles south of Cedar City. It is administered jointly with Zion National Primeval Park, but has not yet been made accessible to the general public.

We Need Wilderness

By SIGURD OLSON

Wilderness to the people of America is a spiritual necessity, an antidote to the high pressure of modern life, a means of regaining serenity and equilibrium.

I have found that people go to the wilderness for many things, but the most important of these is perspective. They may think they go for fishing or the scenery or companionship, but in reality it is something deeper. They go to the wilderness for the good of their souls. I sometimes feel as though they had gone to another planet from which they can watch with cool detachment the fierce and sometimes meaningless scurryings of their kind. Then when the old philosophy of earth-oneness returns to them, they realize that once again they are in tune with sun and stars and all natural things, and with that knowledge comes happiness and contentment.

I believe this need of wilderness is inherent in most of us, even those seemingly farthest removed from it by civilized living. The cities may cover it up, make us forget temporarily; but deep underneath is an inherent urge for naturalness.

City life is artificial. Because artificiality leads to a sense of unreality and frustration, unhappiness often results. That is the price a people pays for high technological success, and that is the reason an intelligent, thinking people knows that unless it can break away and renew its contact with a slow-moving natural philosophy, it will lose its perspective and forget simplicity and wholesomeness.

In recognition of this now almost general need of our people, the National Park Service, the U. S. Forest Service, and the various states have wisely set aside many areas that may be classed as wilderness—areas dedicated to the spiritual welfare of all. Yet we see commercial interests constantly at work, backed by powerful lobbies—interests calling for the cutting of the last stands of virgin timber, the exploitation of the last untouched reserves of the continent. They make the preservation of wild country a battle, and place the comparatively small reservations we have, in constant jeopardy. This element in our population makes necessary the utmost vigilance on the part of government agencies in charge of our parks and forests, as well as on the part of those organizations that understand what is at stake. The reservations already created are woefully inadequate to meet the need and give to the people of all parts of the United States the opportunity of wilderness recreation. This is especially true in the large centers of population; yet it is here that the need is greatest and opposition strongest.

One highly encouraging aspect of the wilderness problem is the realization that as a nation we are approaching cultural maturity. No young nation ever worries overmuch about the intangible assets of wilderness as long as its great battle is to subdue wilderness and carve out cities and roads and farms from the wild. Now, for the first time, we are able to look back and see where our mistakes and short-sighted policies have brought us. We can see that we have squandered a national heritage of beauty and wealth and have only a few places left to remind us of the continent's past primeval glory.

We know now just how valuable these fragments of the old America have become to us as a people. We see them in a new light and realize that in addition to being museum pieces of the past, they are vital to our happiness, and they are investments in national character.

To give the people of this country an opportunity to renew their old associations as a race, to find themselves and their real qualities, to rejuvenate their spirits through simple living in the out-of-doors, is the real purpose of the preservation of wilderness.

Origin of the Standards

IN the early days of national park establishment, certain aspects of the national policy governing the establishment and preservation of the parks were generally accepted by the federal government and the people. Almost from the beginning, however, there were threats to the integrity of the system. As a consequence, in 1923, a declaration of policy known as *National Park Standards* was formulated in conformity with the ideas of former Secretary of the Interior Franklin K. Lane and Stephen T. Mather, first director of the National Park Service. It was written by a sub-committee of the Conservation Committee of the Camp Fire Club of America, and was endorsed by nearly a hundred organizations interested in the function, use and preservation of the national parks.

In 1944, owing to changing conditions of later years, particularly with regard to increased pre-war travel and improved transportation, which affected the national parks, the Executive Committee of the National Parks Association felt that the policy statement on standards for the great national parks should be restudied and, if possible, clarified and strengthened.

A sub-committee of the Association's Executive Committee was therefore appointed to make such a study and offer recommendations for improvement. This sub-committee presented the result of its study to the Association's Board of Trustees at its annual meeting in May, 1945. From this, a revised version of the standards emerged, which was later endorsed by numerous organizations throughout the country.

"Primeval"

An important change in the revised standards statement was the addition of the word *primeval* in the title. The use of the word was in accord with the Association's previous suggestion to include a descriptive word in the names of those parks whose dominant characteristic is landscape substantially untouched from primeval centuries.

During many years, the Association has urged official adoption of such a term. The reasons for so doing are obvious and compelling. The great national parks that have been set aside to preserve outstanding examples of scenic grandeur in a setting of unspoiled nature are, in their essential characteristic, in a class by themselves, and are entitled to a special designation. Such a designation for this group of reservations would conform to the nomenclature of other groups of reservations that are administered by the National Park Service, such as national *historical* parks, national *military* parks, national *capital* parks and national *battlefield* sites. Of still greater importance, it would help to make clear in the public mind the purpose of the reservations, and it should reduce the political assaults constantly being made upon them. Official adoption of the term will require an Act of Congress.

There are many people in this country who crave the wilderness and its values more than anything else in the world.—ROBERT MARSHALL

To many Americans the worth of a region is measured by the dollars that it will produce, but more and more people are coming to feel that regions may possess valuable characteristics that are not to be measured in dollar bills.
GEORGE BIRD GRINNELL

The National Park Service and the Standards

By NEWTON B. DRURY, Director

National Park Service

WHEN, a quarter of a century ago, a group of conservation stalwarts drafted the first *National Park Standards*, they were influenced, in some degree, no doubt, by the earlier policy pronouncement of May 13, 1918, of Secretary of the Interior Franklin K. Lane. That these conservationists possessed knowledge of national park problems and that they had an appreciation of National Park Service ideals is evidenced by the soundness of their proposals for building and maintaining a National Park System. To bring the original *Standards* up-to-date has required but slight modification.

The 1945 revision of the 1923 *Standards* by the National Parks Association was occasioned by the increased travel of Americans to their vacation lands. Concurrent with this greater use, there arose a need for further study of the demands for "improvement" of roads in the national parks and the proposals for expanded facilities needed to keep up with the demands of visitors. Inasmuch as the revised statement clarifies and strengthens the earlier statement of policy in these respects, it is a timely document that should be distributed widely.

Proposals for the development and use of the national parks and monuments must be aligned with defined objectives of the National Park Service. It is the purpose of the Service to hold development and use within a pattern that will give to visitors the most satisfying experience that the areas can provide without material impairment of natural and historical characteristics. The "enjoyment" envisioned in the act creating the National Park Service is refreshment of mind and spirit as well as physical refreshment, and for that reason development for recreational use (*i.e.*, outdoor sports) must be subordinated to the preservation and interpretation of the significant natural and historical features. The physical recreational use is an important by-product, but one which must not be permitted to affect adversely the primary use of the national parks and monuments.

National Primeval Park Standards gives emphasis to this policy and points again to the fact that the national parks and monuments are justified as a part of the nation's conservation program insofar as they hold intact natural landscapes, scientific phenomena, wildlife and historical treasures of such importance as to serve great national interests.

Maintain these standards and we shall preserve one of the noblest institutions in the world—one that no other nation can rival. Fail to maintain them and the upbuilding of more than half a century will be lost, perhaps within a decade.—Robe t Sterling Yard, first executive secretary, National Parks Association.

Proposed parks are measured by the standards set by the major national parks of the system. As long as these standards shall prevail, there is no danger of too many national parks being established, or of the excellence of the present system being lowered.—Stephen T. Mather, first director, National Park Service.

National Primeval Park Standards

A DECLARATION OF POLICY

1. Definition

NATIONAL PRIMEVAL PARKS are spacious land and water areas essentially in their primeval condition and in quality and beauty so outstandingly superior to average examples of their several types as to make imperative their preservation intact and in their entirety for the enjoyment, education and inspiration of all the people for all time.

It follows:

1. That primeval park areas must be of national importance to warrant their commitment to national care.

Mount Rainier in Mount Rainier National Primeval Park.—No commercial use or activity such as logging, mining, grazing or damming of water courses is permitted on primeval park lands.

Department of the Interior

2. That the area of each primeval park must be a comprehensive unit embracing all territory required for effective administration and for continuing representation of its flora and fauna.

3. That each primeval park area shall be a sanctuary for the scientific study and preservation of all animal and plant life originally within its limits, to the end that all native species shall be preserved as nearly as possible in their aboriginal state.

4. That wilderness features within any primeval park shall be kept unmodified except insofar as the public shall be given reasonable access to outstanding spectacles.

5. That with respect to any unique geological formations or historic or prehistoric remains within its confines, each primeval park shall be regarded as an outdoor museum, the preservation of whose treasures is a sacred trust.

6. The educational and spiritual benefits to be derived from contact with pristine wilderness are of prime importance to all people, and call for the existence and vigilant maintenance of primeval park areas by responsible government agencies.

7. That primeval parks must be kept free from commercial use, and that sanctuary, scientific and inspirational uses must always take precedence over non-conforming recreational uses.

II. Recommended Policy

The areas to be included in the national primeval park group must conform to the standards for such parks herein set forth. Areas that may be added to this group must be units that will fully maintain or increase its supreme scenic magnificence, its scientific and educational superiority, and its character as a unique national institution.

It is desirable that, as a general principle, national primeval parks should differ as widely as possible from one another, and the National Primeval Park System should represent a wide range of typical areas of supreme quality.

To preserve the National Primeval Park System, it must be recognized: (1) that any infraction of standards in any primeval park constitutes an invasion of the system; (2) that the addition to the system, as a national primeval park, of any area below standard lowers the standard of the system. Every proposed use of any primeval park in defiance of national primeval park standards, and the admission to the system of any area falling short of the standards must be resisted. Areas primarily of local interest must not be admitted to the National Primeval Park System.

III. Legislation

1. Procedure: The first official act toward the creation of a national primeval park is usually the introduction of a bill in Congress. Since the beginning of the system in 1872, according to established precedent, the bill is referred to the Public Lands committees of Senate and House. These committees in turn refer it to the Secretary of the Interior for a report on the standards and availability of the proposed park. The Secretary of the Interior in due course refers the bill to the National Park Service for examination of the area and for a report to him. The Secretary embodies the recommendations of the National Park Service in his report to the Congress which is then in position to take action. Public hearings are often held by the appropriate committees prior to making their reports to the Congress.

2. Recommendations: (1) The examination of an area to determine its suitability as a primeval park should be made at the expense of the federal government and not at the expense of the local community which would benefit by the park's creation. Committees to consider boundary problems should be strictly advisory to the federal administration to which alone they should be empowered to report. (2) Exact metes and bounds

Pronghorn antelope in Yellowstone National Primeval Park.—Each primeval park area shall be a sanctuary for the preservation of all animal life originally within its limits, to the end that all native species shall be preserved as nearly as possible in their aboriginal state.

based upon studies made by the National Park Service should be established by Congress in the organic act creating every new park. The federal government should purchase, as soon as practicable, alienated areas within the boundaries of an existing primeval park, and also areas necessary to round out such park. (3) No steps affecting an existing primeval park or concerned with the creation of a new primeval park should be taken without a prior study and approval of the National Park Service which alone possesses the requisite knowledge, tradition and experience united with responsibility to the people. No area offered for the creation of a new primeval park should be considered by Congress until a study has been made of the area by the National Park Service and its recommendations secured. On the recommendation of the National Park Service, park areas should be extended so as to include feeding grounds for the wildlife found therein. (4) Appropriations should be adequate to enable the National Park Service to protect existing parks and their forests against fire, vandalism and other agencies of destruction, and to maintain the system in accordance with national primeval park standards. (5) All existing national primeval parks now up to the standards set forth should remain as created, subject to modification only upon the favorable recommendation of the Secretary of the Interior and the Director of the National Park Service, based upon expert investigation.

IV. Administration

In administering national primeval parks it is recommended:

1. That each park be administered with the primary objective of conserving its highest scientific and inspirational usefulness to the people of the nation.

2. That no commercial use or activity such as logging, mining, grazing or damming of water courses should be permitted on primeval park lands, by exchange or otherwise.

3. That scientific, educational and inspirational values dictate the major uses of primeval parks.

4. That attracting crowds for the sake of records or profits, and the introduction of non-conforming recreational activities be regarded as violations of the national primeval park standards.

5. That scientific administration be applied to all phases of park maintenance, and particularly to the preservation of wilderness, wildlife, and geological features.

6. That a suitable educational program be developed by the National Park Service, using the natural features of the parks as instructional material. The National Park Service should inform the public concerning park purposes and functions, and emphasize the necessity of caring for and protecting irreplaceable objects of natural and scientific interest. No visitor to a primeval park area should leave without having been informed about the special significance of that particular area, as well as of the system as a whole.

7. That roads be developed in each national primeval park only in order to bring the people in touch with its principal features and for the purpose of protecting the park. In every instance they should be constructed and placed so that they will cause the least possible impairment to natural features. Wilderness, sanctuary and research areas should be reached by trail only.

8. That public airplane landing fields, as well as railroad stations, be located outside park boundaries. Flying across national primeval parks, if permitted at all, should be closely regulated.

9. That park buildings be as unobtrusive as possible, harmonizing with their surroundings. They should be erected only where necessary for the protection of the parks and for the comfort of visitors, and at locations where they will least interfere with natural conditions.

10. That concessions be granted only for such business as is necessary for the care and comfort of visitors, and then in definitely localized areas. Such concessions should not interfere with the rights of individuals under park rules to provide for themselves while visiting the parks.

11. That the use of any primeval park interfere as little as possible with the rights of future generations to enjoy nature unmodified.

National Monuments

These standards should apply also to national monuments that are of similar character and purpose as the national primeval parks.

Nature Reservations Abroad

CONVENTION ON NATURE PROTECTION AND WILDLIFE PRESERVATION IN THE WESTERN HEMISPHERE

THE Convention on Nature Protection in the Western Hemisphere came into force for the United States, Guatemala, Venezuela, El Salvador and Haiti on May 1, 1942, and since then for the Dominican Republic, Mexico, Ecuador, Argentina, Nicaragua and Peru.

The American Committee for International Wildlife Protection believes that this Convention, along with the London Convention for African Nature Protection (1933 and 1936), should serve as a basis for discussions which will lead to the establishment of a world convention to further nature protection through international cooperation among all nations. Steps to accomplish these results should be carried out within the framework of the United Nations, or in close cooperation with them.

The Convention on Nature Protection and Wildlife Preservation in the Western Hemisphere covers a broad virgin field for international agreement. This treaty was designed to meet certain international wildlife problems of the twenty-one American Republics. The Pan American Convention establishes a basic pattern for a scheme of parks and reserves throughout the Americas on a basis which experience has proved to be sound. It calls for appropriate protective laws for threatened flora and fauna and it favors cooperation in scientific field studies, the protection of migratory birds, the protection of vanishing species, and the control of contraband fauna or flora protected by the laws of other countries.

Preamble to the Convention

The governments of the American Republics, wishing to protect and preserve in their natural habitat representatives of all species and genera of their native flora and fauna, including migratory birds, in sufficient numbers and over areas extensive enough to assure them from becoming extinct through any agency within man's control; and

Wishing to protect and preserve scenery of extraordinary beauty, unusual and striking geologic formations, regions and natural objects of esthetic, historic or scientific value, and areas characterized by primitive conditions in those cases covered by this Convention; and

Wishing to conclude a Convention on the protection of nature and the preservation of flora and fauna to effectuate the foregoing purposes, have agreed upon the following Article 1:

Description of terms used in the wording of this Convention.

1. The expression *National Parks* shall denote:

Areas established for the protection and preservation of superlative scenery, flora and fauna of national significance which the general public may enjoy and from which it may benefit when placed under public control.

2. The expression *National Reserves* shall denote:

Regions established for conservation and utilization of natural resources under government control, on which protection of animal and plant life will be afforded in so far as this may be consistent with the primary purposes of such reserves.

Kruger National Park in South Africa is the world's largest wildlife reservation, being nearly as large as Maryland. Zebra and wildebeest, as well as lions and many other species, are protected here from gunners for the pleasure of thousands of people who come annually. To visit Kruger is to experience one of the greatest thrills on earth.

3. The expression *Nature Monuments* shall denote:

Regions, objects, or living species of flora or fauna of esthetic, historic or scientific interest to which strict protection is given. The purpose of nature monuments is the protection of a specific object, or a species of flora or fauna, by setting aside an area, an object, or a single species, as an inviolate nature monument, except for duly authorized scientific investigations or government inspection.

4. The expression *Strict Wilderness Reserves* shall denote:

A region under public control characterized by primitive conditions of flora, fauna, transportation and habitation wherein there is no provision for the passage of motorized transportation and all commercial developments are excluded.

THE LONDON CONVENTION FOR THE PROTECTION OF AFRICAN FAUNA AND FLORA

The London Conference was called by invitation of the government of Great Britain, and was held in the House of Lords in late October, 1933. It was in reality a revival of the London Convention of 1900 on the same subject, which unfortunately was never ratified. A resolution calling for another such Convention was passed at the International Congress for the Protection of Nature which was held in Paris in 1931.

Accredited representatives came to London from all the countries having territories on the African continent—the Union of South Africa, Belgium, the United Kingdom of

Great Britain and Northern Ireland, Egypt, Spain, France, Italy, Portugal, and the Anglo-Egyptian Sudan—and there were present through invitation "observers" from the Netherlands, India and the United States.

The spirit in which the terms of a treaty are accepted is often more important than the actual wording of the text, and let us hope that the fine spirit shown at London will be remembered and will point the way to a very real co-operation in international wildlife matters before it is too late. The London Convention went into effect on January 14, 1936. A further conference on the subject was held in May 1938, also in London.

Of the many accomplishments of the Convention, none are more important than those which define and recommend the four types of parks and reserves in Article 2 of the Convention as follows:

1. The expression "national park" shall denote an area (a) placed under public control, the boundaries of which shall not be altered or any portion be capable of alienation except by the competent legislative authority, (b) set aside for the propagation, protection, and preservation of wild animal life and wild vegetation, and for the preservation of objects of esthetic, geological, prehistoric, historical, archeological, or other scientific interest for the benefit, advantage, and enjoyment of the general public, (c) in which the hunting, killing, or capturing of fauna and the destruction or collection of flora is prohibited except by or under the direction or control of the park authorities.

In accordance with the above provisions facilities shall, so far as possible, be given to the general public for observing the fauna and flora in national parks.

2. The term "strict natural reserve" shall denote an area placed under public control, throughout which any form of hunting or fishing, any undertakings connected with forestry, agriculture, or mining, any excavations or prospecting, drilling, levelling of the ground, or construction, any work involving the alteration of the configuration of the soil or the character of the vegetation, any act likely to harm or disturb the fauna or flora, and the introduction of any species of fauna and flora, whether indigenous or imported, wild or domesticated, shall be strictly forbidden; which it shall be forbidden to enter, traverse, or camp in without a special written permit from the competent authorities; and in which scientific investigations may only be undertaken by permission of those authorities.

It is our hope that as the London Convention becomes effective in helping to solve the African problem, similar measures may be undertaken by governments controlling other parts of the world, where no such convention exists, notably in central Asia, India, Siam, Indo-China, Malaya, the East Indies and the Pacific island area.

For Further Reading

The titles listed here are standard works, but a number of them are out of print. They should be available at public libraries and through secondhand book dealers.

SPECIFIC AREAS

ACADIA NATIONAL PARK, ITS ORIGIN AND BACKGROUND, by George B. Dorr, 1942. May be obtained from Mrs. Floyd Sylvia, Bar Harbor, Maine.

CARLSBAD CAVERNS OF NEW MEXICO, by A. W. Anderson. *Cavern Supply Co.*, Carlsbad, New Mexico.

CRATER LAKE, by Howel Williams. *University of California Press*, Berkeley, 1941.

DEATH VALLEY; THE FACTS, by W. A. Chalfant. *Stanford University Press*, Palo Alto, 1936.

DISCOVERY OF THE YOSEMITE, by Lafayette H. Bunnell. *Fleming H. Revell*, New York, 1892.

DISCOVERY OF YELLOWSTONE PARK, 1870, by Nathaniel P. Langford. *J. E. Haynes*, St. Paul, 1923.

ENCHANTED LAKE, by Stanton C. Lapham. *Gill Co.*, Portland, Oregon, 1931.

FIRST THROUGH THE GRAND CANYON, by John W. Powell. *Outing Publishing Co.*, New York, 1915.

GLACIER NATIONAL PARK, Marius R. Campbell. *Government Printing Office*, Washington, D. C., 1914.

GRAND CANYON COUNTRY, by M. R. Tillotson and Frank J. Taylor. *Stanford University Press*, Palo Alto, 1935.

GREAT SMOKIES AND THE BLUE RIDGE, edited by Roderick Peattie. *Vanguard Press*, New York, 1943.

LORE AND LURE OF SEQUOIA, by Herbert E. Wilson. *Wolfer Printing Co.*, Los Angeles, 1928.

LURE OF THE GREAT SMOKIES, by Robert Lindsay Mason. *Houghton Mifflin*, New York, 1927.

MAMMOTH CAVE OF KENTUCKY, by Horace C. Hovey. *Morton and Co.*, Louisville, 1912.

ONE HUNDRED YEARS IN YOSEMITE, by Carl P. Russell. *Stanford University Press*, Palo Alto, 1931.

PREHISTORIC MESA VERDE PUEBLO AND ITS PEOPLE, by J. W. Fewkes. Smithsonian Institution Annual Report, 1916: 461-488. *Government Printing Office*, 1917.

RAINBOW CANYONS, by E. T. Scoyen and Frank J. Taylor. *Stanford University Press*, Palo Alto, 1931.

ROAMING IN HAWAII, by Harry A. Franck. *Frederick A. Stokes*, New York, 1937.

ROCKY MOUNTAIN NATIONAL PARK, by Enos A. Mills. *Doubleday, Page*, New York, 1931.

STORY OF YELLOWSTONE GEYSERS, by Clyde Max Bauer. *J. E. Haynes*, St. Paul, 1937.

THE TETONS, by Fritiof M. Fryxell. *University of California Press*, Berkeley, 1938.

VALLEY OF THE TEN THOUSAND SMOKES, by Robert F. Griggs. *National Geographic Society*, Washington, D. C., 1922.

WILDERNESS OF DENALI (Mount McKinley National Park), by Charles Sheldon. *Scribners*, New York, 1930.

Separate booklets on each national park and on most national monuments are obtainable free from the National Park Service, Chicago 54, Illinois. In addition, a separate 16 page booklet on each national park is obtainable for ten cents apiece from the Superintendent of Documents, *Government Printing Office*, Washington, D. C.

GENERAL

AMERICAN CONSERVATION, by Ovid Butler. *American Forestry Association*, Washington, D. C., 1941.

AMERICA'S NATURAL WEALTH, A Story of the Use and Abuse of Our Resources, by Richard Lieber. *Harpers*, New York, 1942.

ARIZONA'S NATIONAL MONUMENTS, edited by Dale S. King. *Southwestern Monuments Association*, Santa Fe, 1946.

BOOK OF THE NATIONAL PARKS, by Robert Sterling Yard. *Scribners*, New York, 1939.

OUR FEDERAL LANDS, by Robert Sterling Yard. *Scribners*, New York, 1928.

CALL OF THE MOUNTAINS, by LeRoy Jeffers. *Dodd, Mead*, New York, 1922.

CONSERVATION OF AMERICAN RESOURCES, by Charles N. Elliot. *Turner E. Smith Co.*, Atlanta, 1940.

CONSERVATION IN THE UNITED STATES, by A. E. Gustafson. *Comstock Publishing Co.*, Ithaca, 1944.

GLIMPSES OF OUR NATIONAL MONUMENTS, edited by Isabelle F. Story. *Government Printing Office*, 1941.

GLIMPSES OF OUR NATIONAL PARKS, edited by Isabelle F. Story. *Government Printing Office*, 1941.

LET'S GO TO THE PARKS, by Raymond C. Morrison and Myrtle E. Huff. *Wilkinson Printing Co.*, Dallas, 1937.

NATIONAL PARKS OF THE NORTHWEST, by Martelle W. Trager. *Dodd, Mead*, New York, 1939.

NATURAL PRINCIPLES OF LAND USE, by Edward H. Graham. *Oxford University Press*, New York, 1945.

OH, RANGER! A Book about the National Parks, by Horace M. Albright and Frank J. Taylor. *Dodd, Mead,* New York, 1946.

OUR COUNTRY'S NATIONAL PARKS, by Irving H. Melbo. Two volumes. *Bobbs Merrill,* Indianapolis, 1941.

OUR NATIONAL PARKS, by John Muir. *Houghton Mifflin,* New York, 1901.

PIONEER PHOTOGRAPHER, by William H. Jackson and Howard R. Driggs. *World Book Co.,* Yonkers, 1929.

RESEARCH AND EDUCATION IN THE NATIONAL PARKS, by Harold C. Bryant and Wallace W. Atwood, Jr. *Government Printing Office,* 1936.

ROAMING THE ROCKIES, by John T. Faris. *Farrar and Rinehart,* New York, 1930.

ROMANCE OF THE NATIONAL PARKS, by Harlean James. *MacMillan,* New York, 1939.

SEEING THE FAR WEST, by John T. Faris. *Lippincott,* Philadelphia, 1920.

SOIL CONSERVATION, by Hugh H. Bennett. *McGraw-Hill,* New York, 1939.

SON OF THE WILDERNESS (Life of John Muir), by Linnie Marsh Wolfe. *Knopf,* New York, 1945.

THAT VANISHING EDEN (Florida), by Thomas Barbour. *Little, Brown,* Boston, 1944.

YOUR NATIONAL PARKS, by Enos A. Mills. *Houghton Mifflin,* New York, 1917.

WRITINGS OF JOHN MUIR, edited by W. F. Bade. Sierra Edition, ten volumes. *Houghton Mifflin,* New York, 1916-1924.

FAUNA

BIRDS OF DENVER AND MOUNTAIN PARKS, by Robert J. Niedrach and Robert B. Rockwell. *Colorado Museum of Natural History,* Denver, 1939.

BIRDS OF MASSACHUSETTS AND OTHER NEW ENGLAND STATES, by Edward Howe Forbush. Three volumes. *Commonwealth of Massachusetts,* Boston, 1925-1929. The colored plates may be obtained in a separate volume.

BIRDS OF THE PACIFIC STATES, by Ralph Hoffman. *Houghton Mifflin,* New York, 1927.

FADING TRAILS, The Story of Our Endangered Wildlife, edited by Charles N. Elliot. *MacMillan,* New York, 1942.

FAUNA SERIES. National Park Service, *Government Printing Office.*

    No. 1. PRELIMINARY SURVEY OF FAUNAL RELATIONS IN NATIONAL PARKS, by George M. Wright, Joseph S. Dixon and Ben Thompson, 1932.

    No. 2. WILDLIFE MANAGEMENT IN THE NATIONAL PARKS, by George M. Wright and Ben Thompson, 1943.

    No. 3. BIRDS AND MAMMALS OF MOUNT MCKINLEY NATIONAL PARK, by Joseph S. Dixon, 1938.

    No. 4. ECOLOGY OF THE COYOTE IN THE YELLOWSTONE, by Adolph Murie, 1940.

    No. 5. THE WOLVES OF MOUNT MCKINLEY, by Adolph Murie, 1944.

FIELD GUIDE TO THE BIRDS, by Roger Tory Peterson. *Houghton Mifflin,* New York, 1939.

FIELD GUIDE TO THE WESTERN BIRDS, by Roger Tory Peterson. *Houghton Mifflin,* New York, 1941.

FUR-BEARING MAMMALS OF CALIFORNIA, by Joseph Grinnell, Joseph S. Dixon and Jean Linsdale. Two volumes. *University of California Press,* Berkeley, 1937.

HANDBOOK OF LIZARDS, by Hobart M. Smith. *Comstock Publishing Co.,* Ithaca, 1946.

HANDBOOK OF THE BIRDS OF THE WESTERN UNITED STATES, by Florence Merriam Bailey. *Houghton Mifflin,* New York, 1917.

INTERNATIONAL PROTECTION OF WILDLIFE, An Examination of Treaties and Other Agreements for the Preservation of Birds and Mammals, by S. S. Hayden. *Columbia University Press,* New York, 1942.

LIVES OF GAME ANIMALS, by Ernest T. Seton. Four volumes. *Doubleday, Doran,* New York, 1929.

MAMMALS OF EASTERN UNITED STATES, by W. J. Hamilton, Jr. *Comstock Publishing Co.,* Ithaca, 1943.

MEETING THE MAMMALS, by Victor H. Cahalane. *MacMillan,* New York, 1943.

OUR VANISHING WILDLIFE, by William T. Hornaday. *Clark and Fritz,* New York, 1913.

THIRTY YEARS WAR FOR WILDLIFE, by William T. Hornaday. *Scribners,* New York, 1931.

WILD ANIMALS OF THE ROCKIES, by William M. Rush. *Harpers,* New York, 1942.

WILDLIFE CONSERVATION, by Ira N. Gabrielson. *MacMillan,* New York, 1941.

WILDLIFE REFUGES, by Ira N. Gabrielson. *MacMillan,* New York, 1943.

FLORA

BIG TREES, by Walter Fry and John R. White. *Stanford University Press,* Palo Alto, 1930.

BIG TREES OF THE GIANT FOREST, by George W. Stewart. *A. M. Robertson,* San Francisco, 1930.

CACTI OF ARIZONA, by Lyman Benson. *University of Arizona,* Tucson, 1947.

DESERT WILD FLOWERS, by Edmund C. Jaeger. *Stanford University Press,* Palo Alto, 1941.

FEATURES OF THE FLORA OF MOUNT RAINIER NATIONAL PARK, by J. B. Flett. *Government Printing Office,* 1921.

FERNS AND FLOWERING PLANTS OF HAWAII, by Otto Degener. *Honolulu Star-Bulletin*, Honolulu, 1930.
FERNS AND FLOWERING PLANTS OF ISLE ROYALE, MICHIGAN, by Clair A. Brown. *Government Printing Office*, 1937.
FIELD BOOK OF COMMON MUSHROOMS, by W. S. Thomas. *G. P. Putnam's Sons*, New York, 1936.
FLORIDA WILD LIFE, by Charles T. Simpson. *MacMillan*, New York, 1932.
FORESTS AND TREES OF THE WESTERN NATIONAL PARKS, by Harold E. and Virginia L. Bailey. *Government Printing Office*, 1941.
FORESTS OF CRATER LAKE NATIONAL PARK, by John F. Pernot. *Government Printing Office*, 1916.
FORESTS OF MOUNT RAINIER NATIONAL PARK, by Grenville F. Allen. *Government Printing Office*, 1916.
FORESTS OF YOSEMITE, SEQUOIA AND GENERAL GRANT NATIONAL PARKS, by Cary L. Hill. *Government Printing Office*, 1928.
GIANT SEQUOIAS OF CALIFORNIA, by Lawrence F. Cook. *Government Printing Office*, 1942.
HOW TO KNOW THE FERNS, by F. T. Parsons. *Scribners*, New York, 1927.
KNOWING YOUR TREES, by G. H. Collingwood. *American Forestry Association*, Washington, D. C., 1947.
PLANTS OF GLACIER NATIONAL PARK, by Paul C. Standley. *Government Printing Office*, 1926.
PLANTS OF ROCKY MOUNTAIN NATIONAL PARK, by Ruth E. Ashton. *Government Printing Office*, 1933.
PLANTS OF YELLOWSTONE NATIONAL PARK, by Walter B. McDougall and Herma A. Baggley. *Government Printing Office*, 1936.
REDWOODS OF COAST AND SIERRA, by James C. Shirley. *University of California Press*, Berkeley, 1937.
TREES AND FLOWERS OF YELLOWSTONE NATIONAL PARK, by F. E. A. Thone. *J. E. Haynes*, St. Paul, 1929.
TREES OF YOSEMITE, by Mary Tresidder and Della T. Hoss. *Stanford University Press*, Palo Alto, 1932.
WILD FLOWERS, by Homer D. House, *Macmillan*, New York, 1935.
WILD FLOWERS OF THE GREAT SMOKIES, by J. L. Caton, author and publisher, Knoxville, 1940.
YOSEMITE FLORA, by Harvey M. and Carlotta C. Hall. *Paul Eder*, San Francisco, 1912.

GEOLOGY

FOSSIL FOOTPRINTS FROM THE GRAND CANYON, by Charles W. Gilmore. *Smithsonian Institution*, Washington, D. C., 1926-1928.
FOSSIL FORESTS OF YELLOWSTONE NATIONAL PARK, by Frank H. Knowlton. *Government Printing Office*, 1928.
GEOLOGIC HISTORY OF THE YOSEMITE VALLEY, by François E. Matthes. *Government Printing Office*, 1930.
GEOLOGIC STORY OF THE ROCKY MOUNTAIN NATIONAL PARK, by Willis T. Lee. *Government Printing Office*, 1917.
GEOLOGICAL HISTORY OF THE YELLOWSTONE NATIONAL PARK, by Arnold Hague. *Government Printing Office*, 1928.
GEOLOGY OF THE YELLOWSTONE NATIONAL PARK, by Arnold Hague, *et al.* 893 pages. *Government Printing Office*, 1899.
GEYSERS OF THE YELLOWSTONE NATIONAL PARK, by Walter H. Weed. *Government Printing Office*, 1928.
GLACIAL FEATURES OF JACKSON HOLE, WYOMING, by Fritiof M. Fryxell. *Augustana Book Concern*, Rock Island, Illinois, 1930.
MOUNT MCKINLEY REGION, ALASKA, by Alfred H. Brooks. *Government Printing Office*, 1911.
MOUNT RAINIER AND ITS GLACIERS, by François E. Matthes. *Government Printing Office*, 1922.
ORIGIN OF THE SCENIC FEATURES OF GLACIER NATIONAL PARK, by Marius R. Campbell. *Government Printing Office*, 1921.

The following periodicals contain excellent articles on the national parks and monuments:

AMERICAN FORESTS. Published monthly by The American Forestry Association, 919 Seventeenth Street, N. W., Washington 6, D. C.
AUDUBON MAGAZINE. Published bimonthly by the National Audubon Society, 1000 Fifth Avenue, New York 28, N. Y.
THE LIVING WILDERNESS. Published quarterly by The Wilderness Society, 1840 Mintwood Place, N. W., Washington 9, D. C.
NATIONAL PARKS MAGAZINE. Published quarterly by the National Parks Association, 1214 Sixteenth Street, N. W., Washington 6, D. C.
NATURE MAGAZINE. Published monthly by the American Nature Association, 1214 Sixteenth Street, N. W., Washington 6, D. C.
EMERGENCY CONSERVATION COMMITTEE, 767 Lexington Avenue, New York 21, New York. Occasional Bulletins.